GEORGE WASHINGTON'S

1791

Southern Tour

For Hilda Snuggs,
Thanks for your leadership
in local history.

Enjoy the Tour!

WARREN L. BINGHAM

War J. Bingh

THE
History
PRESS

Published by The History Press
Charleston, SC
www.historypress.net

Cover image: *Washington's Arrival in Old Salem* by Werner Willis.

First published 2016

Manufactured in the United States

ISBN 978.1.46711.979.5

Library of Congress Control Number: 2015956822

For my brother, Larry, who inspired me to care about old roads and the South.

The 1791 Southern Tour:
Washington's Round Trip from Philadelphia to Georgia

CONTENTS

PREFACE

In American popular culture, people have an inordinate interest in two things about George Washington: were his false teeth wooden and where did he sleep?

I have lectured and offered vignettes about George Washington for twenty years, mostly about his presidential tour of the South. Invariably, someone will ask about his dentures, pining to know—pun intended—if they were wooden. Folks also often ask me specifically about where Washington slept. Others tell me about where they understand the great man once slept or traveled. Some of the claims aren't plausible, but that makes them no less interesting. In a twist, one gentleman told me of a still-operational colonial inn that proudly advertises that "George Washington never slept here—but you can."

Occasionally, the cherry tree story comes up—the "I cannot tell a lie" tale—advanced by early Washington hagiographer Mason Locke Weems. Most folks, but not all, know the cherry tree story is bogus, apocryphal.

Regarding those false teeth, George Washington was blessed in many ways, but he had tough luck with his dental health. By his twenties, he suffered from toothaches and tooth loss. When he became president at age fifty-seven, he had but one real tooth left; he eventually lost that one.

Washington saw a variety of dentists, who were not practicing a well-advanced art in the eighteenth century. He was fitted for several sets of dentures, some utilizing a lead base filled with a mix of animal teeth, human teeth and teeth carved from hippopotamus ivory.

PREFACE

After Washington's death, like any item linked to the great American, his dentures became notable artifacts. The false teeth turned brown with age, taking on the appearance of wood and giving rise to the myth of the wooden teeth. For those interested in seeing Washington's false teeth, historic Mount Vernon has a set on hand. This is all I offer on GW's bite.

This unassuming book is about where Washington traveled and slept, at least on his presidential tour of the South. This is an essay, not a thesis. Though intended as factual, it's meant as light reading for a general audience or for one with a penchant for historical touring.

Notations are not offered except as stated within the text of the narrative. Washington's diary and correspondence, general references and my life experience provide the base knowledge for the book. Those wanting more information will enjoy the suggested reading. Travelers may use the text, map, photographs and the list of Washington's sleepovers to guide their discovery.

I hope readers enjoy learning about Washington's Southern Tour, but I also hope you will be inspired to consider the history and meaning of things along many of the roads and paths that you follow.

ACKNOWLEDGEMENTS

This book represents my decades-long interest in President George Washington's 1791 tour of the South, most especially of his visit to my home state of North Carolina. Over the years, my interest has been encouraged and my knowledge advanced by many professionals, hobbyists, organizations and some whom I have met serendipitously. I am grateful to them all. At the risk of overlooking some, I especially want to acknowledge the following organizations and individuals:

Augusta Museum of History, Augusta, Georgia; David Anderson, archivist, George Washington University, Washington, D.C.; Boyce Ansley, the Mount Vernon Ladies' Association, Mount Vernon, Virginia; Bob Anthony, North Carolina Collection of UNC–Chapel Hill, Chapel Hill, North Carolina; Erica Backus, Savannah Chamber of Commerce, Savannah, Georgia; Joyce Baker and Elizabeth Mitchell, Charleston City Hall, Charleston, South Carolina; Travis Bowman, Charlotte, North Carolina; Andrea Bridge, Farmville–Prince Edward Library, Farmville, Virginia; Dr. John L. Brinkley, Richmond, Virginia; Johanna Brown, Old Salem, Inc., Old Salem, North Carolina; Bruce A. Buckley, Charlotte, North Carolina; Carl Burke, Historic Halifax, Halifax, North Carolina; Meredith Whitt Burns, Savannah, Georgia; Carol Borchert Cadou, George Washington's Mount Vernon, Mount Vernon, Virginia; Camden Archives and Museum, Camden, South Carolina; Dr. Ed Cashin, Augusta, Georgia; Dr. Jerry C. Cashion, Raleigh, North Carolina; Charlotte Mecklenburg Library, Carolina

Room, Charlotte, North Carolina; Dr. Philander Chase, Papers of George Washington, University of Virginia, Charlottesville, Virginia; Dana Cheney and Gale Doggett, Colleton County Historical and Preservation Society, Walterboro, South Carolina; Walter Coles V, Chatham, Virginia; Carmen Courtney, Virginia Executive Mansion, Richmond, Virginia; Joanna B. Craig, Historic Camden Revolutionary War Site, Camden, South Carolina; Dr. Marylee Dilling, Ridgefield, Connecticut; Dr. Benjamin E. Fountain, Cary, North Carolina; Mary Jane Fowler, Rowan Museum, Salisbury, North Carolina; Phyllis M. Giddens, Morris Museum of Art, Augusta, Georgia; Guilford Courthouse National Military Park, Greensboro, North Carolina; Independence National Historical Park, Philadelphia, Pennsylvania; Ann Jones Hampton, Summerville, South Carolina; Susan Hess, Durham, North Carolina; Dr. R. Don Higginbotham, UNC–Chapel Hill, Chapel Hill, North Carolina; Kimberly Hocking, Finch Library, Peace College, Raleigh, North Carolina; Luther H. Hodges Jr., Chapel Hill, North Carolina; John Hopkins, Christ Church Preservation Trust, Philadelphia, Pennsylvania; Kim Huddle, New Bern, North Carolina; Mitchell Hunt, Greensboro, North Carolina; L.L. Irving, Worsham, Virginia; Kent County Public Library, Rock Hall, Maryland; Harry Kent, New Bern, North Carolina; Tracy Kamerer, Flagler Museum, Palm Beach, Florida; Reverend Sandra Kern, Thyatira Presbyterian Church, Salisbury, North Carolina; Cindy Kinder, Kaminski House Museum, Georgetown, South Carolina; Lee Lansing Jr., Dumfries, Virginia; Rabun Alex Lee, Sylvania, Georgia; Gardelle Lewis Jr., Augusta, Georgia; Library of Congress, Washington, D.C.; Ranger Bill Martin, National Park Service, Charleston, South Carolina; Sandy and Deborah McNeill and their pilot Linwood Williams, Whiteville, North Carolina; Rob McRae, property manager, St. Michael's Church, Charleston, South Carolina; John Miller, congregant, Christ Church, Savannah, Georgia; Katherine Byerly Mize, Halifax, Virginia; Erick D. Montgomery, Historic Augusta, Augusta, Georgia; New Bern–Craven County Library, Kellenberger Room, New Bern, North Carolina; Officer John T. Nicholson, Virginia Capitol Police, Richmond, Virginia; Tom Norris, Raleigh, North Carolina; Olivia Raney Local History and Research Library, Raleigh, North Carolina; Audrey Parla, Lancaster Public Library, Lancaster, Pennsylvania; Spanky and June Pleasants, Cartersville, Virginia; H. Douglas Pratt, North Carolina Museum of Natural Sciences, Raleigh, North Carolina; Ruth Gregory Proctor, Halifax, North Carolina; Tom Rabon, Holly Springs, North Carolina; T.R. Revella, Historic Kenmore, Fredericksburg, Virginia; Jovanka Ristic, American Geographical Society, Milwaukee, Wisconsin;

ACKNOWLEDGEMENTS

Betsy Shaw, Raleigh, North Carolina; Eugene Scheel, Waterford, Virginia; Jennifer Scheetz, Charleston Museum, Charleston, South Carolina; Fred Scott, owner, The Wreck Restaurant, Mount Pleasant, South Carolina; Mary Davis Smart, Charlotte Museum of History, Charlotte, North Carolina; Society of the Cincinnati, Anderson House, Washington, D.C.; Richard Starbuck, Moravian Archives South, Old Salem, Inc., Winston-Salem, North Carolina; State Library of North Carolina, Raleigh, North Carolina; Jean Olive Stubbs, Winston-Salem, North Carolina; Helen Taylor, Winnabow, North Carolina; Sarah Love Taylor, Durham, North Carolina; South Carolina Department of Archives and History, Columbia, South Carolina; Mary V. Thompson, George Washington's Mount Vernon, Mount Vernon, Virginia; Jewel Turpin, Capitol of Virginia, Richmond, Virginia; Amy Walker, Pittsylvania County, Virginia; Pauline Watson, Screven County Library, Sylvania, Georgia; J. Allan Whitlock, Hillsborough, North Carolina; Douglas Wilkins, Hickory, North Carolina; Katherine Wilkins, Virginia Historical Society, Richmond, Virginia; Mark Willard, Danville, Virginia; Werner Willis, Charlotte, North Carolina; Officer D.W. Wilmoth, Prince Edward County Sheriff's Office, Farmville, Virginia; Gretchen Witt, Rowan County Public Library, Salisbury, North Carolina; Dolores S. Wood, New Bern, North Carolina; Jon B. Zachman, Greensboro Historical Museum, Greensboro, North Carolina.

Special thanks to George F. Thompson, principal of GFT Books of Staunton, Virginia, who generously offered professional counsel on publishing and editorial advice.

For their generous provision of office space, I am especially grateful to several Raleigh friends, Tom McGuire and Bert Armstrong of Armstrong & McGuire Philanthropic Advisory and to the A.E. Finley Foundation Board of Directors and its president, Bobby Brown. These organizations not only provided a comfortable office, but they also offered a convivial place to see and be seen.

I was inspired throughout this project by UNC–Chapel Hill professor emeritus of history William S. "Bill" Powell and his wife, Virginia, and by Harvard University professor John R. Stilgoe. These folks gave me the original idea for the book, and their influence and encouragement kept me on the path to completion.

J. Banks Smither, my acquisitions editor with The History Press, was always helpful, prompt and pleasant as he led the way to bring this book to print; he was ably assisted by a courteous, attentive and fast-moving team. I am grateful to them all.

ACKNOWLEDGEMENTS

In November 1793, George Washington wrote to his twenty-something nephew Howell Lewis offering the following advice: "The habit of postponing things is among the worst in the world." Alas, as one who struggles mightily with the habit of postponing things, I am eternally grateful for the love, wisdom and patience—and prodding—from my wife, Laura, who, like Washington, believes in getting things done. Plus, Laura has driven many miles and taken notes and photographs during our considerable touring; she's even cheerfully agreed to take back roads at my request even when a four-lane was nearby. Even Washington wasn't blessed with such a splendid aide-de-camp.

Thanks to all who have informed, cheered and joined my effort. You have made the journey productive, fun and entirely satisfying.

Chapter 1

GEORGE WASHINGTON

GREAT MAN AND FREQUENT TRAVELER

In the spring of 1791, President George Washington traveled round-trip from Philadelphia to Georgia. The trip of nearly 1,900 miles was possibly the longest overland trip made in the history of the American states to that time. But the first president was not seeking any sort of travel record; he had other things in mind. The high mileage came with his mission: a proper visit to the southern states.

I first heard of Washington's Southern Tour in a history class during my senior year at UNC–Chapel Hill when William Powell, a renowned scholar of North Carolina history, shared several anecdotes on Washington's passage through my home state of North Carolina. As Powell told stories of Washington's stops in places I knew, such as Charlotte, Salisbury and Wilmington, George Washington came alive.

Until this revelation, I found George Washington to be so remote and from such another time that he seemed more mythical than real—think Paul Bunyan, the lumberjack of folklore. But when I visualized a tired, aching and nearly sixty-year-old Washington plugging away on a long journey that passed within fifty miles of my hometown, he became human and flesh and blood. For me, George Washington was for sure a living, breathing heroic action figure. Since that day in college, I have been fascinated with the first president and his famed Southern Tour.

For his singular leadership in the establishment of the United States of America, Washington is known as the father of this country. Though his life remains celebrated today, it is important to grasp that Washington was truly a remarkable legend in his own time—and his time was exclusively of the eighteenth century. He died in his home, Mount Vernon, at age sixty-seven in mid-December 1799.

Washington's achievements were magnanimous. As commander in chief, he led the Continental army to victory over the British in the American Revolution, then he presided over the Constitutional Convention in 1787 and, finally, he established the presidency, setting the style and standards for the office. For nearly a quarter of a century, George Washington was the most prominent American, a hero at home and around the world.

George Washington was a dignified man who generally maintained a military bearing. Sometimes he could be formal, aloof and stern, believing that familiarity bred contempt and disrespect. Washington kept his emotional distance from almost everyone. No one called him George; he was General Washington even to his wife, Martha.

Despite his reserved style and personality, a distinctive aspect of Washington's presidency was the vigor with which he connected with the American people. The president and his wife each held weekly receptions, or levees, to receive the public, leaders and elected officials. President Washington and his family often rode on horseback or in a carriage out among the people. And just over two years after becoming president, Washington had visited all thirteen states, a momentous accomplishment given the travel challenges of the time.

Until the twentieth century, Washington indeed saw more of what was his United States than did any other president. During his life as a surveyor, real estate speculator, Virginia militia officer, commander of the American army and a public servant for his state and country, he saw the colonies and states like few others of his time. The old saw "George Washington slept here" is trite, but it is often true. For example, according to one of his biographers, Washington slept in 280 houses during the Revolution alone.

To sleep in so many places required Washington to be on the move, and he was in steady circulation via a variety of conveyances from his mid-teens until his retirement from the presidency in 1797 at age sixty-five. He walked; rode horses; boarded ships, boats and rafts; paddled canoes; and settled into a variety of wheeled carts and carriages. His travels not only took him to the first thirteen states but also to parts of the future states of Maine, Ohio, West Virginia and, likely, Vermont.

Almost all of Washington's travels were confined to the footprint of colonial America; unlike many of the gentlemen of his era, he never traveled to Europe, not even to his ancestral homeland of England. Perhaps if his father had not died when Washington was only eleven, George would have been sent to England for school like his elder half-brothers.

But Washington's opportunities to travel abroad were limited by financial and practical circumstances related to responsibilities to his widowed mother, Mary, and to his siblings. Not only did he not go to England for school, but his mother also refused to let him see the world by joining Britain's Royal Navy. American history might be very

George Washington took an extended trip to Barbados when he was nineteen—his only trip outside the United States. *Painting by Walter Kerr Cooper.*

different if it were not for Mary Ball Washington's obstinacy on keeping her son out of the British navy.

Washington's only trip outside his country was a visit to Barbados, a voyage taken in 1751 at age nineteen with his half-brother, Lawrence, who was nearly fourteen years older than George. Lawrence was not well, a sufferer of tuberculosis seeking relief in what was considered the therapeutic Caribbean climate. George idolized Lawrence, who had been essentially a surrogate father, and he readily agreed to accompany his brother. The brothers were not on spring break; in fact, they left during the fall.

The Washington brothers were away nearly four months, counting rough ocean voyages both ways. The outcome of the trip was mixed: Lawrence's health did not improve, and George contracted smallpox. By the trip's end, George had survived and was forever immune from the pox (a disease that later ravaged his Continental army), and for the first time, he experienced a truly new land, new soil, new vegetation and different customs and manners. And he saw the theater for the first time, which would remain a lifelong interest. This was Washington's only opportunity to do what we now call "study abroad."

During the next three to four decades, Washington grew from young man to American hero. From Lawrence, he inherited the estate, Mount Vernon, greatly improving it. He married the wealthy widow Martha Dandridge Custis and became guardian of her two children. During the American Revolution, Martha proved to be a remarkable and resilient mate for the on-the-go Washington, often joining him in army camps.

Though Washington was neither worldly nor formally educated and had neither visited European capitals nor sailed the distant seas, thanks to his domestic exploits, fine character and good fortune, he was elected the first president of the United States.

Wearing a simple brown suit of wool spun by a Connecticut manufacturer, George Washington, the consummate American, was sworn in as president on April 30, 1789. The inauguration was staged on Wall Street in Lower Manhattan in New York City, the temporary seat of the U.S. government. George and Martha, the much celebrated Virginians, settled in New York.

Just days after taking the oath of office, the new president signaled his intention to visit the thirteen states. In a letter to Vice President John Adams dated May 10, 1789, Washington outlined nine points about the presidency, requesting Adams's consideration and thoughts. Point eight read:

> *Whether, during the recess of Congress, it would not be advantageous to the interests of the Union for the President to make the tour of the United*

States, in order to become better acquainted with their principal characters & internal circumstances, as well as to be more accessible to numbers of well-informed persons, who might give him useful informations and advices on political subjects.

Shrewd and practical, Washington was well aware of his considerable popularity and influence. Touring the states would allow him to meet the American people and to see their circumstances while promoting the Constitution and new federal government. Historian Richard Norton Smith calls Washington's presidential touring an effort "to see and be seen." Additionally, it would provide the physical exercise that he relished and allow him to get away from the office. After all, Washington was an outdoorsman, a surveyor, a soldier and a farmer.

Except, perhaps, in his role as a military officer, George Washington did not especially inspire or captivate audiences with words. Unlike, say, Franklin, Jefferson and Madison, he did not espouse great thoughts or philosophy in either spoken or written form, but Washington literally stood out in a crowd. Standing nearly six feet and three inches, he was not vanilla. Washington had presence, and he knew it. His influence was certainly enhanced simply by being there.

Though Washington surely wanted to see the country and learn more about its land, activities and people, he also wanted to assert the power and influence of the new federal government. The Constitution was untested and still unpopular with many, particularly among the less powerful and affluent. Washington aspired to rally all Americans to the new government.

President Washington's Tours of the States

April 1789	Virginia, Maryland, Delaware, Pennsylvania, New Jersey, New York
October–November 1789	Connecticut, Massachusetts, New Hampshire
August 1790	Rhode Island
March–July 1791	Pennsylvania, Delaware, Maryland, Virginia, North Carolina, South Carolina, Georgia

After years of British control, erased only by a long and tumultuous war, Americans were generally distrustful of government. The concept of being a United States citizen was not easily grasped by the masses; their personal loyalty went first to their family, then to their locality and, finally, to the state.

People needed assurance that their new federal government was, at least, generally benign if not beneficial.

In his tours of the states, Washington carried the nation's flag to the American people. His presence at once projected both federal strength and national unity. There was no one better to do this than George Washington, the hero of the Revolution. For Americans both north and south, George Washington was their common denominator, a trusted man, a great unifier.

I am unsure how Vice President Adams responded to the president's proposed travel notion, but Washington did indeed visit all of the states. George Washington was a man of action.

Washington accomplished his thirteen-state travel venture in three big trips, plus a side trip to Rhode Island. Ultimately, Washington's passage from Mount Vernon to New York City for his inauguration in April 1789 proved to largely satisfy his appearance in the middle states: Maryland, Delaware, Pennsylvania, New Jersey and New York. Along the way, Washington was seemingly surprised at the ceremonial recognition and adulation at stops in Baltimore, Wilmington, Philadelphia, Trenton, Elizabethtown and New York City.

The following fall, Washington staged a tour of New England with stops in Connecticut, New Hampshire and Massachusetts, but Rhode Island had

This coach, now kept at Mount Vernon, is similar to the one used on the Southern Tour. It belonged to Washington's friend, Samuel Powel of Philadelphia. *Author's collection.*

not yet ratified the Constitution, so Washington excluded the small state from his itinerary. By the summer of 1790, Rhode Island finally joined the Union when its cautious leaders had gained assurance that a Bill of Rights would be a part of the Constitution. To pay his respects to the thirteenth state, Washington sailed from New York up the Long Island Sound in August 1790 to approach Rhode Island from its Atlantic Coast. Ironically, the smallest state was the only state that rated an express trip by the president. Little Rhody even enjoyed a bonus high-ranking visitor, Thomas Jefferson, who was then secretary of state.

The ink was barely dry on Rhode Island's endorsement of the Constitution when the national capital moved from New York City to Philadelphia during the fall of 1790. Congress had designated the City of Brotherly Love, where both the Declaration of Independence and the Constitution were crafted, to be the temporary national capital until 1800, by which time a permanent seat of government, a new federal district, would be identified and prepared.

In March 1791, Washington launched his last swing through the states from present-day Center City, Philadelphia. The Southern Tour, as it became known, was the longest trip, stretching to Georgia by way of Virginia and the Carolinas. It marked Washington's first ever visit to a state south of Virginia, the only exception being Washington's probable visit within North Carolina's portion of the Great Dismal Swamp while on surveying expeditions during the 1760s.

The Great Dismal exists today and remains impressive, but it has been significantly altered, drained and reduced in size during the last 225 years. In Washington's day, it was a behemoth, daunting and wild wetland straddling the border between southeastern Virginia and northeastern North Carolina.

Regardless of where Washington tramped and floated within the isolated swamp, it would hardly constitute a worthy visit to North Carolina. One legend goes that during his time in the Great Dismal, Washington may have spent a night or two at Eagle Tavern in Hertford, North Carolina, but such a stay is undocumented.

At times, Washington's tours were simple, understated affairs with limited fanfare and protocol, but on occasion, and especially in the larger communities, aspects of Washington's presidential visits resembled an English Royal Progress, those occasions when traveling monarchs got out among their people, toured the country and were honored lavishly and, well, royally.

During the Southern Tour, Washington was fêted and celebrated in myriad ways—bells pealed, cannons fired, parades rolled, toasts were offered and dinners and dances sometimes went late into the night. Leading the

The Southern Tour rolled down sections of the King's Highway in the Carolinas. Several relatively unaltered and unpaved stretches of the eighteenth-century road can be found in Lowcountry South Carolina. *Author's collection.*

ceremonies and entertainment were elected officials, militia and their officers and two organizations of which Washington was a member, the Freemasons and the Society of the Cincinnati, the latter being the military officers of the Revolution. Less privileged citizens were exposed to the president, too. Likely awed by the mere prospect, they lined the dusty roads and pushed through crowded town centers when news came of George Washington's presence in town.

But the journey was not all grand and glorious. The entourage faced many challenges inherent to travel during the early American republic. They endured rutted and blocked roads and suffered from heat, choking dust and drenching rain. Routes and directions were confusing, and signs were few and far apart, but well-meaning local guides and ceremonial escorts sometimes slowed the entourage and served to stir up dust with their horses' hooves.

Crossing water was time consuming and dangerous. On occasion, at the end of long, tough days, Washington was resigned to stay in poor lodgings. In general, the roads and public taverns were worse in the South than elsewhere in the country. The president worried constantly about the condition and welfare of his horses—his transportation. Some days were simply monotonous and tiring.

Washington's cavalcade was small but impressive as it rolled along over the clay and sand of the South. The appearance of Washington's gleaming white carriage pulled by four horses was a head-turner. The entourage included a baggage wagon pulled by two horses. At least four other well-kept steeds came along as spare mounts, including Washington's tall white charger Prescott.

Eight men made the trip—a ninth started the journey but took ill and made it no farther than Mount Vernon. The coachman and attendants were dressed in red livery, while President Washington and his traveling secretary, William Jackson, dressed as gentlemen, sometimes in their military uniforms. Jackson, a South Carolinian, was an officer during the Revolution and had first served Washington as secretary of the Constitutional Convention. Among several secretaries on the president's staff, Jackson had already traveled with Washington on the tour through New England.

The Southern Tour kept the president away from Philadelphia for three and a half months. During the trip, Washington paid two visits to Mount Vernon; saw parts of seven states; established the site of the future Washington, D.C.; traveled from sea level to nearly one thousand feet in elevation; visited with five governors; and saw a number of battlegrounds of the Revolution.

In his presidential travels, George Washington gained an education from the land and the people, and from his presence, the people gained a sense of being Americans. The price of uniting the nation required considerable time and patience from its president, along with his endurance of saddle sores and choking dust.

Chapter 2

ME AND WASHINGTON'S
SOUTHERN TOUR

I was born and raised in the Piedmont of North Carolina—the red rolling land of the mid-state that connects the flat Coastal Plain with the Appalachian Mountains. Except for six years in Virginia during the 1990s, I have lived my entire life in North Carolina.

After college, I began my career in state government, later moving to business, where I was happily employed for many years in sales with an insurance company. My work unit provided services to banks and lending institutions throughout the eastern United States.

In a sales role, I traveled to meet with clients and prospects, many of whom golfed, hunted, fished or played tennis within their business relationships. Clues to the avocations of bankers in small southern towns are often on prominent display in their offices. In addition to photographs and mementoes, I recall that some rural bankers even kept golf clubs and fishing gear in the corners of their offices. In central Virginia, I called on a banker who enjoyed hunting; a stuffed bobcat mounted over his credenza glared at all who dared enter his workspace.

I flailed and failed at golf, unable to understand any mechanical differences between my occasional good shots and the numerous awful ones. My limited interest in hunting and fishing didn't persist past my early teens, and though I can play a little tennis, I have never been competitive against well-practiced players.

The vivid description by friends who have experienced the ocean swells, putrid smells and frequent sea-sickness associated with deep sea fishing has kept me on the dock, and though I have enjoyed some awkward and clumsy sailing, I have barely escaped concussions from blows from the boom. Alas, without interest or skill in the traditional sporting avocations, I sought means to distinguish myself with my clients, a way to enhance and deepen relationships with those bankers outside of their offices.

I fell in love with American history in elementary school, and by high school, I had developed an interest in public speaking. The thought of combining these interests gave me an idea. I decided to become proficient on a couple of history topics and offer to bring programs to my clients' civic clubs; it seemed every banker was in a civic club. Soon I began to research and develop two talks: the United States' purchase of Alaska and George Washington's Southern Tour of 1791.

In January 1992, I enrolled in a public speaking course offered by Duke University's Continuing Studies. The class met on Duke's East Campus, roughly thirteen miles from the UNC classroom where, years earlier, I had first heard of Washington's Southern Tour. As a final project, each participant in the public speaking course was expected to give a fifteen-minute presentation in front of the class. For my class final, I gave my first ever talk on George Washington's Southern Tour; I still have the tape of that presentation. The talk felt good: I had fun and the audience enjoyed it. It was a solid kickoff to a new hobby.

Twenty years later, I have spoken on the Southern Tour hundreds of times. The vast majority of the talks have been given in North Carolina and a few in neighboring states. I have presented some public lectures but mostly have spoken to a variety of civic clubs, book clubs, heritage groups and professional associations. In tribute to my old professor and friend William Powell, who died in 2015, I try to make George Washington come alive for every audience. In the 1990s, Professor Powell heard me speak on the Southern Tour a couple times. What a treat for me; I even made him laugh.

The study of the Founding Fathers is in vogue these days, and generally, my audiences embrace "George Washington" as a topic. The "Alaska" talk never went over as well, never felt as good, and I quit giving it after only a few runs. An understanding of George Washington is foundational to being American, whereas the acquisition of Alaska is but a building block in American history. Most Americans feel a need to try to understand George Washington.

For years now, I've been vigilant for information and insight on Washington's travels, especially on the Southern Tour. A lot of people offer me anecdotal information. Others ask me if George Washington visited their town during the Southern Tour. They are fascinated with

North Carolina features a number of historical markers commemorating the Southern Tour. A few years ago, the author spoke in Tarboro on the anniversary of Washington's visit to the town. *Author's collection.*

Washington's travels, especially with his treks near their community. They tell me of how they have heard he slept at this place or stopped at that place. Such curiosity is healthy. You can learn a lot by understanding the America that Washington knew. The study of his travel informs our understanding of both time and place of the eighteenth century.

Many smile when they hear of Washington's travels, often laughing about the "George Washington slept here" thing. Some raise their eyebrows and suggest that it was all of that travel, all that "sleeping around" that really made Washington the father of his country. Though some contemporaries of Washington suggested that he had a pretty good sense of humor, I doubt he would have liked that joke. History indicates that though George Washington was indeed a frequent traveler, his movements were honorable, often noble.

Some have considered Washington's travels in fun and entertaining ways. On July 25, 1932, pilot Jimmy Doolittle, accompanied by a great-great-great-grandniece of George Washington, flew to every part of United States where George Washington traveled. An impressive daytrip in 1932! Certainly an important aspect of this stunt for Doolittle was to demonstrate the wonders of the airplane. The high flying was one of many activities that year to commemorate the 200th anniversary of Washington's birth.

Also in 1932, the National Geographic Society developed an attractive poster-sized map depicting the routes and places of Washington's lifetime travels. *Travels of George Washington* is still produced and even is available in laminate. Now, wouldn't George Washington appreciate the sturdiness and durability of a laminated map?

A 1930s cartoon strip, "George Washington's Travels," written by James W. Brooks with art by Calvin Fader, was published in newspapers around the nation. It was a serious serial on early American history, definitely not humorous, delivering brief historical messages in a very dull way. But perhaps youngsters were drawn to the illustrated strip more readily than to a book or article.

In 1940, playwright Moss Hart unveiled *George Washington Slept Here*, a play about an old, falling-down farmhouse where, of course, George Washington might have slept. The play was followed in 1942 by a movie adaptation by the same name. Jack Benny and Ann Sheridan starred in the movie, a release that Warner Brothers billed as a riot, a comedy riot that is. However, the play and movie did not create a riot at the box office. Though these presentations were only moderately successful, they did further inculcate "George Washington slept here" as part of American culture.

In addition to sleeping here and there, Washington also made numerous stops in his travels without pulling off his boots. He halted for many reasons: meals, refreshments, meetings and, certainly, many breaks to rest, water and feed his horses. Through the generations, families pass along lore of their ancestors' encounters with Washington. Luther Hodges, the son of a popular former North Carolina governor of the same name, includes a story in his personal memoir about how his ancestor met Washington in South Carolina during the Southern Tour.

STATES VISITED DURING WASHINGTON'S SOUTHERN TOUR
*1790 Population and Rank Among the Thirteen States**

Pennsylvania	434,373 (2)
Delaware	319,728 (6)
Maryland	59,096 (13)
Virginia	691,737 (1)
North Carolina	393,751 (3)
South Carolina	249,073 (7)
Georgia	82,548 (11)

*Numbers in parentheses represent the states' rank among the thirteen states

Indeed, it was my discovery of Washington's travels in North Carolina that made the great man truly relevant in my life. By the time I was in college, I was steeped in knowledge of the Atlantic South and of early American history—the Southern Tour was a fascinating microcosm of both subjects.

My appreciation of the tour is rooted in my life experience and education; I saw many of the places along the route of the Southern Tour during childhood, much of the eastern United States has been on my life's itinerary, the same places that Washington visited or knew.

My father and a cousin, both Tar Heel natives, left North Carolina in their late teens, around 1930, for adventure and employment in Washington, D.C. Despite the Great Depression, they found work at an A&P grocery store. Forever after, my dad was a fan of Washington, D.C. (and of A&P). Dad regularly hauled our family through Virginia on sightseeing vacations to the nation's capital. Those trips sometimes included stops in Petersburg, Richmond, Fredericksburg, Mount Vernon and Alexandria, all part of Washington's Southern Tour.

Dad also carried us all over the Carolinas and Virginia on mountain and beach vacations and to visit family. Aunts, uncles and cousins lived all about the three states. My ancestors have lived in the region since the mid-1700s.

Many stops of Washington's tour have always been a part of my life. Charlotte was a destination for shopping and dining, especially back when the Queen City featured malls and restaurants quite different from those in my small hometown. My dad arranged business loans from a Salisbury bank; as a kid, I joined him on jaunts to the bank, memorable trips that often included a stop at a barbecue joint. And among several high school church youth trips, one delivered me to historic Center City Philadelphia, the site of Washington's home at the time of the Southern Tour.

As a Boy Scout, I camped at Myrtle Beach and otherwise have often visited the Grand Strand. Just out of college, I joined a good friend for a memorable trip from Raleigh to Charleston in an open-top Fiat Spider. In the early 1960s, my family enjoyed visits to a then new resort, Hilton Head Island, South Carolina, and nearby Savannah, Georgia. And over several summers during my high school and college years, I drove a delivery truck all over the Carolinas. All of these wanderings placed me near the route of Washington's Southern Tour.

I boarded a railroad car pulled by a bright green engine of the Southern Railroad for my first ever train trip—a short ride with my kindergarten class from Salisbury to Concord; my mother was among the class escorts. Washington traveled between those places in late May 1791, except he was escorted by his retinue and local militia instead of by his mom. On my next train trip thirty years later, I traveled to Petersburg, Richmond, Fredericksburg, D.C. and Philadelphia—all part of the Southern Tour.

In the months following college graduation, my first ever airplane flight was aboard a Piedmont Airlines turbo-prop DC-3 from Wilmington, North Carolina, to D.C. The flight was on a bright, sunny day. I recall looking out the window and seeing the landscape for the first time from an aerial perspective. Most of us now take flying for granted, but it is good to remember how airplanes—despite any hassle or inconvenience—wondrously carry us over mountains, rivers and many topographic challenges confronting travelers of yore. In 1791, George Washington spent sixteen days traveling between Mount Vernon and Wilmington, a distance of around 370 miles; my first airplane flight covered it in less than two hours.

With a fondness for the early highways, I have driven U.S. 1 from Key West to Baltimore and U.S. 64 from middle Tennessee to the North Carolina Outer Banks. I enjoy seeing things on foot, so I have pretty much walked Manhattan from stem to stern and have enjoyed long hikes in the Blue Ridge Mountains and in the Green Mountains of Vermont. I've often been a happy pedestrian in the Southern Tour towns of Charleston, Savannah, Augusta, Columbia, Richmond, Annapolis and Washington, D.C. Old trails, old highways, little-used streets and old buildings excite me; they are our ever-present connections with the past.

I've been in the vicinity of every place Washington ever visited—plus many more. I am even on a long, slow course to visit all fifty state capitol buildings. However, of Washington's travels, certainly I know the places of the Southern Tour the best.

Though I have never followed the circle of the Southern Tour in a single trip, I have been along or near the entirety of Washington's route—some areas many times—even including brief sails on the Chesapeake Bay, Charleston Harbor and Savannah River. For the past twenty years, I have been especially aware of my travels near the route of the Southern Tour, and recently, I have made a concerted effort to see all sections of it.

In most places, I do not know the specific road or Washington's exact route, and in some cases, it seems nigh impossible to know those things with certainty. Many roads from 1791 are not intact, at least not in long stretches. Local history buffs sometimes know roads and Washington's routes or probable routes, but even among them there can be confusion and disagreement as to where roads once laid and about which ones Washington would have used.

Long before this country store was built in rural Virginia, Washington passed somewhere near here on the way from Charlotte Courthouse to Prince Edward Courthouse (now Worsham). *Author's collection.*

In my adult travels, I have always been an observer, even if only through the windshield. I especially enjoy learning some history and geography of the places I visit. Historical markers—history on a stick—are my friends. Signs identifying creeks and rivers are informative and, to me, intriguing. Observant travelers will note certain redundancy in names, such as the many waterways named Deep Creek and Little River. I wonder about the names, their origins and if there are any connections between them. I find such observation and reflection good for the soul. If time allows, I live more for the journey than the destination.

George Washington—a surveyor, farmer, soldier, outdoorsman and politician—was surely observant of places he passed. His diary entries often noted the type of trees and soil, the health of the crops, the depth of rivers and the appearance of buildings. We should all at least occasionally be as observant as Washington. He is a role model for paying attention to your surroundings and learning from it. For reasons of health, safety and self-instruction, I suspect most travelers of early America were much more aware of what was around them than are modern travelers.

Early in my research of the Southern Tour, I discovered the one big treatment ever done on the subject, a handsome well-illustrated book published in 1923, *Washington's Southern Tour 1791* by Archibald Henderson. Henderson was a North Carolina native and an outstanding professor of mathematics at UNC. He grew up in Salisbury, and it was there that his prominent ancestor Congressman John Steele was among those hosting Washington in 1791.

Professor Henderson was exceedingly bright, clearly a genius. I am not sure when the phrase "Renaissance man" came into use, but Henderson fits the tag. Beyond his scholarship in mathematics, he wrote on matters of science, history, drama and literature. Henderson took a deep interest in Irish playwright George Bernard Shaw and collected materials on him, went to Ireland to meet him and became his biographer. His significant collection on Shaw is now in Yale University's archives.

Henderson was a big proponent of the history of his native state and of the University of North Carolina, which was his undergraduate alma mater and longtime employer. He produced a thorough book on the buildings and grounds of UNC in which he gave the history of campus construction from dormitories and classrooms to boilers and playing fields. He wrote histories on his Episcopal churches in Salisbury and Chapel Hill. Along the way, I hear he played a pretty good game of tennis. (His late son by the same name is in the North Carolina Tennis Hall of Fame.)

In a 1935 article in the *Richmond Times-Dispatch*, Dr. H.J. Eckenrode, director of the Division of Archaeology and History of the State of Virginia, said, "In my judgment, Archibald Henderson, of the University of North Carolina, is the leading Southern intellectual of this age. One of the foremost writers on the modern drama, he has also done historical work of a high order. His volume, *Washington's Southern Tour*, is one of the most interesting books dealing with the father of the country."

In *Washington's Southern Tour*, Henderson does not always distinguish between documented history and folklore. Though his profile of Washington is certainly hagiographic, it is a very worthy book—with footnotes adding considerable context, especially with biographical information on the people who Washington encountered on the trip.

The single most important resource on the Southern Tour is a publication of a primary source—volume six of *The Diaries of George Washington*—compiled and edited by staff of the Papers of George Washington at the University of Virginia. Volume six includes the transcription plus the editors' marvelous, insightful footnotes of the special diary that Washington kept daily during the tour. The diary runs from March 21 through July 4, 1791.

The larger part of Washington's actual Southern Tour diary is in the collection of the Virginia Historical Society (VHS) in Richmond. For some reason, at some point, the diary was split in two—March 21 through June 1 wound up in Richmond. However, the diary's pages from June 2 through July 4 are at the Library of Congress in Washington.

James Keith Marshall, a grandson of Chief Justice John Marshall, donated the bigger portion of the diary to the VHS on December 21, 1859, almost exactly sixty years after Washington's death. Justice Marshall was a friend and biographer of Washington's; I speculate that Bushrod Washington, George's nephew who inherited Mount Vernon, gave the diary pages to Justice John Marshall, after which they eventually wound up with his grandson. Alas, "Jimmie" Marshall, a graduate of Virginia Military Institute, was just twenty-four in July 1863 when he died at Gettysburg as a Confederate officer.

On a trip to Richmond, I arranged to see the diary at VHS. The librarian placed it on a study table in the main reading room. Wide-eyed, I viewed Washington's small journal with excitement and reverence.

At first, I stood over the diary, before taking a seat in front of it. I was not allowed to touch the thin booklet of yellowed pages measuring 7 inches by 4 7/8 inches, but the librarian carefully showed me a few of Washington's entries. I imagined those pages in Washington's hands as he made his way on the Southern Tour. What a small but important artifact from such a large life. And what a treat for me to see!

James Keith Marshall apparently donated the diary as loose pages. But at some point long ago, it was bound in a dark-brown Morocco grain cloth, a form of goatskin leather. The words "Washington's Diary" are stamped in gilt. Blessedly, the diary has survived for a long time and even managed to come out of war-torn Richmond unscathed after the Civil War. It is interesting that both sections of the diary wound up in places on the Southern Tour itinerary—Richmond and Washington, D.C.

The smaller diary at the Library of Congress covering the last month of the tour apparently was part of a large set of Washington's papers that were maintained by Washington's heirs—a line of nephews—and sold by the mid-1800s to the federal government, technically to the Department of State. The State Department transferred its collection of Washington's papers to the Library of Congress in the early 1900s. I have yet to lay eyes on the diary section kept in D.C.

Travelers of Washington's era are to be admired for their spirit, strength, bravery and patience. Such was required, especially of those

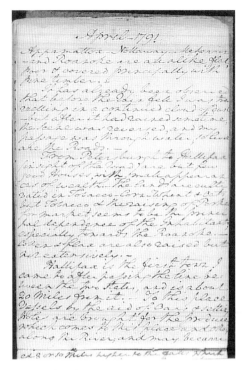

Washington kept a daily diary during the Southern Tour. *Courtesy of the Virginia Historical Society.*

who set forth over unfamiliar routes to unknown places. My idea of intrepid travel is going more than twenty miles from home in my unreliable twenty-year-old Jeep Cherokee. To do so without a fully charged cellphone and my auto club card is especially daunting.

Most of my travel along the route of the Southern Tour has been made in the comfort of late-model automobiles. But, hey, President Washington also traveled as comfortably as anyone possibly could—for 1791 that is, which is an important qualifier.

George Washington got his country up and running; he sustained the United States and was the necessary glue that brought disparate places and people together. His leadership paved the way for the rest of American history, both the good and the bad. In my estimation, the first president is clearly the most important, if not the greatest, of the American presidents. By sharing my knowledge of his Southern Tour, along with many of Washington's personal characteristics, I have engaged and entertained family, friends and many audiences. The Southern Tour has been my device to convey the historical importance of George Washington.

On Sunday, February 20, 1955, the *Raleigh News & Observer*, apparently in tribute to Washington's approaching birthday, published an article, "Washington's Tour Reviewed." It was written by my future professor William S. Powell; I was born the very next day. Perhaps I was predestined to have a fascination for the Southern Tour.

Chapter 3

THE PRESIDENT PLANS THE SOUTHERN TOUR

In September 1790, William Blount, an accomplished and well-connected North Carolinian, stopped by Mount Vernon for an overnight stay on his way to Philadelphia. In the preceding month, President Washington had appointed Blount as governor of the Territory South of the River Ohio, essentially present-day Tennessee. Washington was at home at Mount Vernon, a rarity during his presidency, when Blount called.

Blount relished the visit with the president; the two had first met in 1787 during the Constitutional Convention where Blount had been a delegate from North Carolina. Blount's record was distinguished: he had served in several legislative bodies and had been an officer in the Revolution. He was among the who's who of North Carolina, as was his wife, Mary "Mollie" Grainger Blount, who descended from one of the founders of Wilmington.

In addition to visiting the president to discuss his new role as territorial governor, Blount brought inquiry from North Carolina governor Alexander Martin. Martin anticipated that Washington might be ready to tour the southern states, perhaps even as soon as that fall, and was anxious to know of the president's plans. Martin and leading southerners knew that Washington had already visited all the states except Virginia, the Carolinas and Georgia.

At first, Washington demurred on Blount's notion of a pending visit to the South. The president cited the demands he faced during his brief respite at Mount Vernon and from the ongoing business of the national government. And surely preparation time was needed for the move of the federal capital from New York City to Philadelphia late that year. However, later in Blount's visit, Washington returned to the discussion and indicated that if Congress adjourned before spring, then he would entertain a journey to Virginia, the Carolinas and south to Savannah and Augusta during March, April and May 1791.

Blount was pleased with the news and had to be thrilled to get it directly from the president. Indeed, he apparently was the first one to learn of Washington's intentions. Perhaps Blount's inquiry actually prompted the president to make plans for the Southern Tour.

Shortly after his visit to Mount Vernon, Blount wrote his brother John Gray Blount, who lived in the eastern North Carolina coastal community of Washington. Washington, North Carolina, and Washington, Virginia, each lay claim to being George Washington's oldest namesake community—both are old communities with their own special charm. William Blount told his brother of what he had learned on his visit to Mount Vernon and that he had sent word to Governor Martin on the president's prospective spring visit to the South.

In the letter, Blount offered that Washington would likely take the lower road en route south (traveling the lower elevation along the fall line and Coastal Plain) and take the upper road on his return north (through the Piedmont west of the fall line). Blount waxed on about the prospect of Washington's visit, "I want Mollie and my children to see him for such another man will not appear again in these days." Additionally, Blount encouraged his brother to work with dignitaries and officials in North Carolina to prepare for the president's visit, all the while guarding the specific contents of his letter from the press. William Blount died ten years later in Knoxville, where he had led Tennessee from territory to statehood, but in the fall of 1790 he was the first to know that George Washington was coming to tour the South.

Later that same fall, in November, the federal government moved from New York to Philadelphia; Congress had designated the Pennsylvania city to be the nation's temporary capital until 1800. As the calendar turned to 1791, with the seat of government being at least temporarily resolved, George Washington, the hero of the American Revolution, could focus on the challenge of creating the American presidency.

Five hundred years before Washington led the American republic, Alfonso X was the long-running king of Castile, one of the kingdoms that eventually formed Spain; he is credited with saying, "Had I been present at the creation I would have given some useful hints for the better ordering of the universe."

Taking Alfonso to heart, Washington, who was certainly present at the creation of the United States, was very useful in his role of establishing the presidency and the workings of the government. He developed much of the style and protocol of the presidency, and he established a tradition that lasted over 140 years by relinquishing the office after two terms.

Only the exigencies of the Great Depression and World War II, combined with the ambition of Franklin D. Roosevelt, brought the nation a president who served more than two terms. In 1951, the Twenty-second Amendment to the U.S. Constitution capped the president to a two-term limit, ensuring that future presidents would live up to George Washington's sensibilities.

Washington's leadership style was to be visible, to be seen and to see others. Modern managers might call it "walk around time," where the chief executive regularly meets with or is generally available to his employees, clients and constituents. Washington generally was seen and available in all of his leadership roles—as soldier, planter and president. Especially as president, Washington wanted to be seen by the citizenry, giving confidence that he was in charge yet conveying he was of the people. He did not want to be seen as aloof or as exercising power only behind closed doors; indeed, Archibald Henderson called Washington's tours of the states "democracy on parade."

Washington was busy fighting the Revolution in 1777 when the Continental Congress first developed an American government under the auspices of the Articles of Confederation, a document that gave most of the power and revenue development to the states. Throughout the country, there was a strong distrust of the power and intentions of a centralized national government.

The Articles went into effect in March 1781, but by any standard, the government and relationship between central government and the states was ineffective. There was much jealously between the states; issues such as slavery, taxation and debt payment from the Revolution were divisive.

In early post-Revolution America, the typical citizen was loyal to his family, locality, region or state—not to the new United States. Loyalty to country as we know it today was indeed a new notion. Many referred to their state as their country, and fearful of monarchial trappings, people could not happily imagine a strong central ruler.

Ultimately, enough influential Americans felt that governmental realignment was needed for the good of both the country and the states, and the Articles of Confederation were replaced by the U.S. Constitution in 1787. Yet during his first term as president, Washington was keenly aware that many of the past concerns about central government remained. Nowhere was distrust and uncertainty greater than in the South, with its large population of small farmers and independent craftsmen who generally desired to be left alone.

Given the significant concern about strong rulers and strong governments, George Washington was the solution to the question of who should be the first U.S. president. Washington enjoyed special dispensation among the people. He was a trusted hero. His significant role in the new government was a salve for much of the angst. Yet Washington was the most prominent Federalist, those who believed firmly in the Constitution and a strong central government.

GEORGE WASHINGTON'S CABINET DURING THE SOUTHERN TOUR

Vice President	John Adams
Secretary of State	Thomas Jefferson
Secretary of the Treasury	Alexander Hamilton
Secretary of War	Henry Knox
Attorney General	Edmund Randolph
Postmaster General	Samuel Osgood

The first Congress paid George Washington a whopping $25,000 annual salary, though for the most part, he was responsible for much of the expenses related to his role as president, including the operation of his household. The presidential salary remained at this level until being bumped up to $50,000 in 1873. At first, Washington refused the salary, but Congress insisted on the principle, on which Washington also agreed, that the presidency should not be reserved for only those wealthy enough to work for free.

So, for his travel expenses, Washington often dug into his presidential earnings. Though Washington already personally owned a handsome large coach used in his official appearances and travel as president, as he prepared for the rough roads of the South, he acquired from the Clark Brothers, Philadelphia carriage makers, an additional new chariot. The new chariot was lighter in weight and otherwise designed to better take the abuse of rugged roads. Furthermore, in his travel, Washington generally spurned private hospitality, including lodging, feeling it inappropriate. However, he would find it impractical to pass up some offers of private hospitality during the Southern Tour. On certain days, access to food, lodging and equine provisions were inconvenient, if not unavailable or, often, awful.

The Washington chariot was white or cream in color with a gold frame and undercarriage. It featured folding steps for ease of access, Venetian blinds and images of the four seasons were painted on the doors. The vehicle's four corners displayed the Washington family crest.

Today, it seems the wealthy are often the first to get the latest gadgets, and indeed, Washington, who exemplified wealth and style in his day, had an odometer affixed to the axle. During the Southern Tour, Washington often took note of how many miles his chariot traveled between points.

Travel was hazardous and uncertain throughout the United States but especially in the South. Roads were generally bad—often deeply rutted, muddy, dusty, blocked by downed trees and poorly marked. Horses tired or were injured. Carriages and wagons broke down. Bridges were rare; waterways were forded or crossed via unreliable ferries. If you carried many provisions, they might spoil, yet the food and lodging to be found along the way was bad.

William Loughton Smith, a South Carolina congressman, was a gentleman but was experienced in the rugged ways of the road. Smith, who had accompanied Washington on the 1790 trip to Rhode Island, was coincidentally en route from Philadelphia to his home in Charleston in the spring of 1791. Smith, however, was traveling south on the upper road, and his departure trailed Washington's by several weeks.

Smith kept a travel diary in which he was, at times, humorous or sarcastic, but his account gives quite an impression of the nature of the roads, land, food and lodging. While in south-central Virginia, Smith wrote:

> *I passed this afternoon several small taverns, and traveled an hour after dark to reach Billy George's because it was recommended as the best, but I found it bad enough; there was neither rum nor sugar, he borrowed some rum from a neighbor, but I lost my tea. The bugs made a heartier supper on me than I did on my bacon and eggs; I was glad, however, to find that my horse fared better than I did, and before six the next morning, I proceeded on my journey.*

As he planned his Southern Tour, Washington knew of the potential challenges, the discomfort and inconvenience of travel; he was quite experienced at it. But that said, Washington was now fifty-nine years old and surely was less tolerant of such travail than he once was. As the nation's chief executive, Washington believed in dignifying the office without, of course, looking kingly. There is a big gap between kingly and sleeping with bed bugs, roaches and mosquitos, so Washington sought the happy medium.

Washington enjoyed details and was directly involved in the careful selection of the route of the Southern Tour. His itinerary was shaped and influenced by several factors. The president wanted a representative tour of Virginia, the Carolinas and Georgia, but specifically, he wanted to visit Charleston, South Carolina, then the fourth-largest city in the United States, a place of affluence and influence.

Washington consulted his network of southern friends for suggestions on routes, seeking detail on mileage, water crossings and respectable lodging. North Carolinians William Blount, James Iredell, John Baptista Ashe and Hugh Williamson—respectively a governor, judge, congressman and a former Continental army physician—were among those offering information. It is likely that the aforementioned William Loughton Smith was consulted too.

With the assistance of several secretaries, Washington settled on a route. Notable are some of the communities that were not included on the Southern Tour itinerary. Among the more significant towns missing are Williamsburg and Norfolk in Virginia and Edenton, Washington, Fayetteville and Hillsborough in North Carolina. Some wonder why the president went to Savannah and Augusta but not Atlanta. That is a simple answer: Atlanta was founded in 1837.

Washington's means and style of travel emulated his previous tours. He generally rode in a coach, but he also had a personal horse at the ready. Washington was a great believer in exercise on horseback, and he wanted the option for reasons of appearances and practicality of riding high on horseback. A baggage wagon and some other riding horses were brought along. The president needed a small but competent accompaniment for the rigorous trip over unknown roads to unknown places. From his staff at the president's home in Philadelphia, he selected a secretary, five hired men and two slaves.

In December 1790, Washington fired coachman Arthur Dunn for alcohol abuse; his replacement was Hessian John Fagan. I don't know how well Fagan spoke English, but he proved quite able in handling the coach and horses on the Southern Tour.

To assist the coachman was postilion James Hurley, who would often ride one of the chariot's horses to provide extra stability and guidance. Others selected to make the Southern Tour were John Mauld and Fiedes Imhoff, two footmen who could assist with a variety of chores and errands. William Osborne served as the president's valet.

Two slaves, Giles and Paris, drove the baggage wagon and brought along the extra riding horses. Giles and Paris were Mount Vernon slaves whom the president had brought to Philadelphia. In early March, Giles was sent ahead to Mount Vernon by boat per correspondence between Washington and his nephew and estate supervisor John Augustine Washington.

Washington selected William Jackson, one of his presidential secretaries, as his aide, bodyguard and traveling secretary for the Southern Tour. Jackson was born and partly raised in England before coming to Charleston, where he became a well-established South Carolinian, rising to the rank of major during the Revolution.

Jackson served as secretary to the Constitutional Convention where, of course, he was directly in service to Washington, who was president of the convention. During Washington's tour of New England in the fall of 1789, both Jackson and another secretary, Tobias Lear, accompanied Washington. By the time of the Southern Tour, Jackson seemed perfect for this demanding travel role. He was youthful and strong, just age thirty-two, unmarried and clearly someone with whom Washington felt comfortable. Jackson and Washington were the only gentlemen in the retinue.

The Southern Tour lineup included the presidential chariot pulled by four brown horses (Washington's preferred white horses would be too hard to maintain on the long trip over dusty and muddy roads) and a baggage wagon pulled by two horses. Five additional horses made the trip, including Washington's tall white charger Prescott. Additionally, the president's greyhound, Cornwallis, was along for the ride and run.

As March neared in 1791, George Washington anxiously watched the proceedings of Congress. If he was leaving for the South, he wanted to get going by mid-March in order to time a retreat from the Deep South before the arrival of what he called the "warm sickly months."

Congress adjourned on March 3, 1791, but among its last acts was the establishment of the first direct federal tax, a tax on distilled liquor produced by domestic distillers (imported liquor was already taxed). Washington, supportive of the tax, knew he could soon commence his trip, but now he not only needed to sell southerners on the new federal government but also on the notion of a new tax to help support it.

Ironically, before Washington could even leave town for a final journey to complete his rounds to the thirteen states, Congress admitted Vermont as the fourteenth state, effective March 4, 1791. Additionally, Congress made arrangements for Kentucky to become a state in the summer of 1792.

However, this news had no bearing on Washington's travel plans; he was soon headed south and, in fact, never did pay a visit to Vermont after its statehood. His focus was to finish what he started, a visit to the thirteen original states. This he would do.

Chapter 4

GOING SOUTH

CENTER CITY, PHILADELPHIA, TO NORTH CAROLINA

With Congress adjourned, Washington aspired to embark on the Southern Tour by mid-March, but miscellaneous demands and the preparation to be away until July apparently delayed his start. For one thing, the president had to put into place a system to identify and collect the new tax on liquor. On March 15, he issued an executive order establishing an infrastructure to accommodate the new tax, including the establishment in each state of tax collection districts, or surveys, and tax collectors.

By March 17, Washington made a commitment to depart on Monday, March 21, as revealed in his letter to Daniel Carroll in Maryland, one of the commissioners of the federal district by the Potomac. He wrote, "I have thought best, upon every consideration, to fix on Monday next for the day of my departure from this city [Philadelphia]…which brings it to Monday the 28th of this month, at which time, if no accident intervenes, I shall expect to meet Commissioners at that place [George Town, Maryland]."

All was astir at Philadelphia's 190 High Street, the president's home, on the morning of March 21. Outside the handsome, three-story brick house, finely trimmed with pediment windows and dentil molding, the president's cavalcade lined up and packed for the long journey.

First Lady Martha Washington bid them farewell; she would remain in Philadelphia as the trip was considered much too arduous for a lady. Since he was carrying a good deal of the household staff with him, the president advised Mrs. Washington and his secretary Tobias Lear to hire a housekeeper and cook in his absence.

At approximately eleven o'clock that morning, coachman Fagan roused his horses with the command of giddy-up and the small entourage eased forward. A coach and four, a wagon and two, five other horses, eight men and a greyhound were underway. They wouldn't see 190 High Street again until July 6.

In the saddle that morning and escorting the president to the Delaware border were two cabinet members, Secretary of War Henry Knox and Secretary of State Thomas Jefferson. Jefferson fretted about the performance of the president's coach on the poor roads of the South, fearing it might tip over. As a tip-over preventative, Jefferson advised Washington to lower the hang of his carriage, but Washington preferred to gain stability through postilions mounted on the coach horses.

Washington would be leaving the capital for months. With that in mind, he assiduously reviewed important affairs with all members of his cabinet and busily corresponded on both government and private matters during the month of March through the early weeks after his departure. The cabinet was informed of the president's probable itinerary, which Washington called his line-of-march. Washington would be close to the regular run of the mail through mid-May in Savannah.

However, for four to five weeks during May and June, the president's passage would be away from the flow of regular mail as he traveled into upland Georgia and the Piedmont of the Carolinas and Virginia. Washington offered his itinerary and route to the cabinet, but practically speaking, it would be hard to get a message to the president until his arrival in Fredericksburg, Virginia, in mid-June.

For the citizens and leaders of the young and fragile United States, it was at once a time of calm and fear. The country was a small but growing place with a population of around four million residents scattered from New England to Georgia; the majority of residents lived not far from the Atlantic Coast. The country was at peace, and the first Congress and government under the Constitution were, so far, performing very well. Despite Washington's absence, Vice President John Adams felt good enough about the government that by May he had left Philadelphia for his home in Massachusetts.

Yet underlying the calm were many concerns. The United States perceived threats by Indians, Spain, Britain, France and even pirates at sea. There were concerns about potential uprisings of free blacks, slaves and disenchanted Revolutionary soldiers. Sectional tension between the slave and non-slave states already existed, and there was a general distrust of government.

In an April 4 letter to his cabinet, Washington wrote:

> *I have to express my wish, if any serious and important cases should arise during my absence, (of which the probability is all but too strong) that the secretaries of the departments of state, treasury, and war may hold consultations thereon, to determine whether they are of such a nature as to require my personal attendance at the seat of government—and if they should be so considered, I will return immediately from anyplace at which the information may reach me.*

As Washington was jostled down the hard, rutted roads south of Philadelphia, he knew that, generally, the citizenry had no great sense of identity as Americans or loyalty to the United States. He calculated that his tours would improve the general acceptance of the government and bring a common felicity to the American people. George Washington was the common denominator between all classes of people in all regions. Most people admired and respected Washington; he had the influence to unite the country.

As the late historian Don Higginbotham opined, "Washington embodied the spirit of the American Revolution and the Constitution. From the moment of his appointment as commander-in-chief of the Continental Army until his retirement from the presidency two decades later, George Washington maintained his focus on American unity."

Washington's first days on the road went well enough, but the smooth sailing ended quite literally on the night of Thursday, March 24, on a ferry voyage across the Chesapeake from Rock Hall, Maryland, to Annapolis. Rock Hall on Maryland's Eastern Shore was a well-established point for ferry service to Annapolis, and Washington had crossed there a number of times.

Despite an early arrival in Rock Hall for breakfast that morning, the president's cavalcade could not be accommodated until mid-afternoon due to the lack of appropriate ferry vessels. By three o'clock, a borrowed boat, along with another vessel, was provided. The president's group would have to be split. Washington boarded the borrowed boat, which was the larger of the two. Apparently, a third boat was scheduled for an even later departure that would bring Paris and the last couple of horses across the bay.

The voyage finally was underway, but soon, it was apparent that the crew was unfamiliar with the borrowed sailboat. Washington quickly took notice of it. In annoyance, he penned in his diary, "I was in imminent danger from the unskillfulness of the hands and the dullness of her sailing."

The president's boat struggled for hours in light winds, but things changed from bad to worse as a dangerous storm developed, bringing strong gusty winds, choppy waters and "constant lightning and terrible thunder." As the boat entered the Severn River around ten o'clock, it ran aground on Greenbury Point. Once free, the crew managed no better than to ground it on the opposite side of the river on Horn Point.

In pitch darkness and heavy fog, and no longer even sure where they were, the boat and its crew and passengers, including the president of the United States, remained fast aground until after daybreak on Friday. As the sun came up, all aboard must have been happy to see that they were just one mile from Annapolis. A rescue vessel was on the way to greet Washington. Later that morning, the coachman, Fagan, who had been on the president's boat along with the coach and four, nearly drowned when he fell into the Severn in a calamitous moment involving yet another rescue boat.

Once ashore in Annapolis, the president learned that his traveling companions in the smaller boat from Rock Hall—both men and horses—had arrived safely in Annapolis the night before at eight o'clock. The nasty evening was soon put behind them as the president was welcomed by the firing of fifteen cannons, and the travelers had a chance to recover with two overnights in the Maryland capital. Paris and the last two horses did not arrive from Rock Hall until Saturday.

The festivities in Annapolis were typical of what Washington would experience throughout the tour. The president lodged at Mann's Tavern, just as he had in December 1783 when he resigned his commission as commander of the Continental army. Over the years, Jefferson, Madison and Monroe also lodged at Mann's, as did many others in the inn's long history. Later renamed City Hotel, the former Mann's Tavern survived into the early twentieth century.

Maryland governor John Eager Howard received the president and hosted a dinner and dance in his honor. Fifteen toasts were drunk at the dinner, one of which was "to the perpetual union of distinct sovereign states under an efficient federal head." No doubt, Washington gave that one a rousing huzzah! Each toast drunk was then saluted by the discharge of cannon, leading me to wonder if this early American tradition of combining toasts and cannon fire is the origin of the expression "getting blasted."

Going South

Governors of the Southern Tour

Maryland	John Eager Howard
Virginia	Beverley Randolph
North Carolina	Alexander Martin
South Carolina	Charles Pinckney
Georgia	Edward Telfair

Washington visited St. John's College, where just a year or two later, Francis Scott Key, the future lyricist of "The Star-Spangled Banner," would matriculate. Additionally, the president soon would have a stepson and a couple of nephews enrolled at St. John's. The college thrives today with a curriculum based on the Great Books, and its highest-profile sports competition is a popular annual croquet match with the neighboring U.S. Naval Academy.

The president also visited the Maryland Capitol, circa 1772, a grand building nestled in the middle of today's crowded, hilly downtown Annapolis; the domed structure is perhaps the longest-serving legislative building in the United States. By Sunday, as he left town under the roar of another artillery tribute, the president's attention turned to a different capital, the proposed federal capital on the Potomac. After an overnight in Bladensburg, Maryland, the president's next important business was in George Town, Maryland.

Back in January, Washington had issued an executive proclamation putting forth parameters for the establishment of a "permanent seat of the general government," in other words, a national capital. The proclamation cited both Maryland and Virginia's agreement to cede land to form the new capital.

Washington's proclamation was in response to Congress's Residence Act of 1790, the law that established Philadelphia as the temporary capital for ten years and laid the groundwork for a new capital on the Potomac by 1800. The act gave the president the authority to select the specific site on the Potomac and to appoint commissioners, a surveyor and a planner to lay out and oversee the construction of the new capital, the "residence" of the federal government.

The Residence Act stipulated that the city should not exceed ten miles square. Washington settled on a site exactly ten miles square, placing the new capital between the Anacostia River and Rock Creek, absorbing the Maryland communities of George Town and Carrollsburg, with its southern apex taking in Alexandria, Virginia.

In George Town, Washington met with his appointed federal district commissioners, Thomas Johnson and Daniel Carroll of Maryland and David Stuart of Virginia, at Suter's Tavern. Andrew Ellicott, district surveyor, and Pierre Charles L'Enfant, chief planner, were there, too. The president arrived in George Town on Monday, March 28, and immediately went to work with these important appointees.

Essentially, Washington was chief executive for the development of what he called the "federal city." For a man trained as a surveyor, who liked details and being in charge, Washington must have relished the role. But Washington did not enjoy dissension, disagreement and pettiness, all of which awaited him.

In addition to selecting the site and managing the aforementioned individuals, Washington had to assuage competing private interests among the local citizens along the Potomac and jealousies, particularly between neighboring Maryland communities of George Town and Carrollsburg. It was understood that no new federal buildings would be erected in Virginia's ceded section, where Washington owned land.

After meeting with the commissioners, as well as Ellicott and L'Enfant, Washington not only was brought up to speed on the site and plans, but he also learned more about the concerns and questions among the local residents and landowners. Landowners in George Town and Carrollsburg were apprehensive about the effects of the creation of the capital. They wondered if those effects would be positive or negative. How much land would be needed? How much would the federal government pay the land sellers? Exactly where would the government buildings be placed?

After riding the site of the federal city on the morning of the twenty-ninth, Washington sent word for locals to meet him at Suter's at six o'clock that evening. The first president of the United States was hosting a town hall.

That evening, Washington told the local landowners that their conduct was unbecoming and selfish, counteractive to public purpose. Many locals assumed the new city would encompass a few hundred acres, but Washington—guided by the big-thinking of L'Enfant—advised the audience that the city would be over six thousand acres, taking in all of George Town, Carrollsburg and Alexandria.

After informing a rapt audience that the entire district would be laid out in streets and city lots, the president and planners put forth a plan that required landowners to both sell a portion and donate a portion of any necessary land for the government, quickly pointing out how their remaining land would surely increase in value with the development of the city. Within all of the pronouncements and offers, Washington also made it clear that if suitable arrangements could not be made there on the Potomac, then the capital might just remain in Philadelphia.

Landowners digested and accepted the news and details well, and Washington must have felt accomplished afterward as he joined the federal district leadership for dinner at Uriah Forrest's George Town home. Forrest was a large landowner in the area and had been an officer in the Revolution—and was a good Federalist supporter of Washington's.

Washington was likely cheerful that evening as he broke bread among like-minded dinner companions. It was the close of a good day for the leadership team and for landowners like Uriah Forrest. The following morning, after spending additional time with the commissioner, L'Enfant and Elliott, Washington, knowing the country was on a clearer path to a new national capital, crossed the Potomac for Alexandria and a week's stay at home, Mount Vernon.

The lands of Mount Vernon had been in Washington's family all of his life, and the mansion house had been his home since the mid-1750s. If absence makes the heart grow fonder, Washington was likely a very happy man during this weeklong visit to Mount Vernon. According to Mount Vernon research historian Mary Thompson, Washington was able to visit his beloved estate only twelve times during his eight years as president. Two of the visits occurred during the Southern Tour, as Washington made stops en route south and en route north.

Today, Mount Vernon is a bustling enterprise and America's longest-running restoration and preservation project—and a highly successful one. Thanks to the Mount Vernon Ladies' Association, which acquired the home and some of the surrounding acreage in 1858, not only has the mansion been restored and continuously improved and maintained, but many of Washington's great interests have been carefully and thoughtfully revived and demonstrated. Handling over one million visitors a year, Washington might have to acknowledge that the estate has never been more efficient and productive.

Crops and livestock thrive on Mount Vernon's model farm. Wildlife is encouraged on the grounds; your path might just be crossed by a wild turkey. Something is often blooming in the flower and kitchen gardens, and the beautifully rebuilt greenhouse, which Washington patterned after a similar structure in Baltimore, is full of exotic plants. The exchange of seeds and plants among gentlemen was an important part of eighteenth-century networking; Washington was always anxious to see what he could successfully grow at Mount Vernon, even if only in the greenhouse.

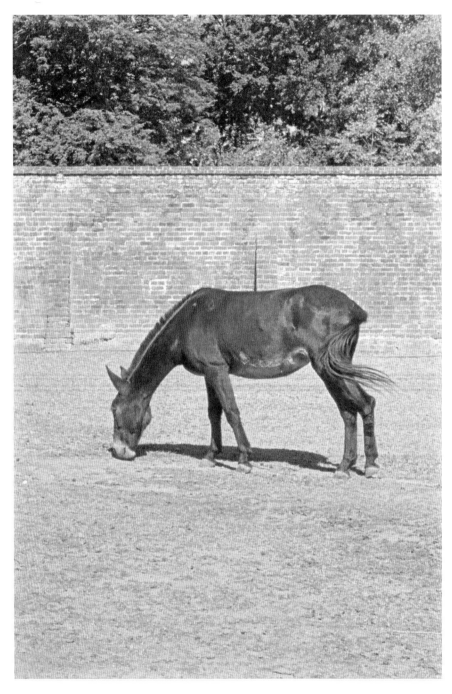

Washington bred mules at his beloved Mount Vernon estate. Today, the site maintains a demonstration farm with livestock. *Author's collection.*

Washington's self-designed octagonal threshing barn, his gristmill and his liquor distillery have been rebuilt. Some slave quarters remain unenhanced, showing the sad and austere conditions they tolerated. All of the restoration has been done with careful attention to historical detail and accuracy. The staff at the distillery have even researched and confirmed that indeed Washington appropriately paid his federal tax on Mount Vernon's distilled spirits.

Complementing its exacting historical preservation, Mount Vernon features a modern orientation and educational center informing visitors about the estate and Washington and his times. And it hosts a variety of lectures and musicales, along with a wine festival. Mount Vernon works closely with schools, teachers and education leaders to promote the memory and meaning of Washington. A beautiful and state-of-the-art research library building opened late in 2013.

Washington quickly settled into a happy and productive reunion with Mount Vernon, announcing for posterity in his diary that from March 31 to April 7, "remained at Mount Vernon visiting my plantations every day." With Mrs. Washington back in Philadelphia, he probably spent most of this time in his study or on horseback examining Mount Vernon's farms, which encompassed nearly eight thousand acres.

Mount Vernon sits high above the Potomac River. The entire river channel is considered within the state of Maryland. *Author's collection.*

Encouraged by how things went in the federal district, Washington turned to other important business, such as composing a letter of condolence to a good friend from abroad, the emperor of Morocco, whose father had died. The United States' longest-running diplomatic ties to this day are with this small North African nation, which accepted the American colonies as an independent nation beginning in 1777.

Scholars estimate that Washington penned up to twenty thousand letters in his life, and he knocked out seven of those missives on April 4, one of those being a letter to his cabinet reviewing his itinerary for April and May. Of course, Major Jackson was there to help. Washington also offered to the cabinet that if any "serious or important" cases arose, he would return from the trip immediately upon their consideration that he should do so.

Meanwhile, just over one hundred miles south of Mount Vernon, U.S. senator Benjamin Hawkins of North Carolina was visiting Petersburg, Virginia, and dipping his pen to write Washington, lamenting that his stay in Petersburg would be over before the president's anticipated arrival there in mid-April. Additionally, the senator shared his observations on the sentiments of North Carolinians toward the national government, opining that the people of North Carolina seemed to be generally in favor of the federal government, but Hawkins cautioned Washington that the anti-Federal forces were virulent.

Specifically, Hawkins advised Washington that North Carolina's anti-Federalist leader Willie (pronounced WY-lee) Jones of Halifax had stated that "he reveres very much the character of General Washington, but that he would not invite the president of the United States to dine with him." In other words, when Washington called on Halifax, Jones would receive Washington as a great man but not as the president. The so-called United States and its president had domestic detractors.

Washington and his band of travelers, minus Giles, resumed the journey south on Thursday, April 7. Giles, suffering from an unspecified illness and physically unable to make the trip, remained at Mount Vernon. Perhaps Giles was already ailing when the president sent him down early by boat from Philadelphia.

Washington's horses fared better than Giles during the respite; the president wrote, "Recommenced my journey with horses apparently well refreshed and in good spirits." The president was always concerned about his horses, and not just because he genuinely honored and respected the beasts but because they were his transportation.

Washington crossed Occoquan Creek near this spot on April 7, 1791. In recent years, the U.S. Board of Geographic Names redesignated this Potomac tributary as Occoquan River. *Author's collection.*

About ten miles from Mount Vernon, the group reached Colchester, a small port and tobacco inspection center on the King's Highway at Occoquan Creek. The community was first settled in the 1750s, and a ferry began operation by the early 1780s. Washington and General Rochambeau, the French general, passed here en route to Yorktown in 1781, but now, ten years later, Colchester was already in decline; however, a ferry over the Occoquan was still in service.

Washington was probably aboard the ferry with his coach and four when one of the horses—still hitched to the coach—was spooked and went overboard into what Washington described as "swimming" water. One by one, the other three horses—all hitched to the coach to some degree—landed in Occoquan Creek while still a good fifty yards from shore.

Amazingly the carriage was not pulled into the creek. Aided by men in small boats and others from the ferry and from shore who dove into the water, the horses were saved as the ferry moved to wading water. Just two weeks removed from the wild sail on the stormy Chesapeake, the travelers were off to a rough start just miles from Mount Vernon. Perhaps it has always been true that most accidents happen close to home, but fortunately, there was no significant injury, loss or damage—just a lot of excitement.

In 1791, with Colchester already in decline, the community of Occoquan, a little farther upstream, replaced it as the area's center of commerce. By the late nineteenth century, what once was Colchester was by then mostly wilderness. Eventually, U.S. Route 1 took over the path of the old King's Highway in this part of Virginia and was conveyed by bridge over the Occoquan. In recent years, George Mason University researchers have done archaeological work in old Colchester, and though the actual community is gone and appears on few maps, the name is still known by some locals and historians.

Washington's next stop was Dumfries, which today claims to be the longest-running chartered town in Virginia. Named for the city in Scotland, Dumfries was settled in the seventeenth century and was chartered in 1749. By the time of Washington's stop, Dumfries was the home of about one thousand souls, including Mildred Washington Lee, the president's niece, with whom he took tea.

Washington's Dumfries lodgings are unknown. Perhaps he stayed with his niece and her husband, lawyer Thomas Lee, or maybe he found a public house. The president's earlier travels to Dumfries surely made him familiar with Williams' Tavern, sometimes known as Love's Tavern, a building from around 1760 that still stands hard by U.S. 1. By the twentieth century, Williams' was known as the Stagecoach Inn, and it was open and receiving guests until about 1950. Today, Williams' houses the Prince William Historic Preservation Foundation.

The travelers went relatively unnoticed on the first couple of days out of Mount Vernon. They were unexpected at the early stops, but as Washington and crew spent a quiet night in Dumfries and an unattended ride to Fredericksburg the following day, they soon would face considerably more attention from mounted escorts, well-wishers and the curious.

Setting out about 6:00 a.m., Washington arrived in Fredericksburg by early afternoon Friday, surprising the citizens of his quasi-hometown and apparently his widowed sister, Betty Washington Lewis, who was maintaining a plantation. It was Washington's first visit to Fredericksburg since becoming president, during which time his mother, Mary, had died in August 1789. She was buried on the Lewis plantation.

Betty Lewis, the widow of Fielding Lewis, with whom she bore eleven children, was an actuarial rarity. In that era, women in the mode of frequent childbirth often predeceased their husbands. Their old home is now known as Kenmore and is open for tour. The grave site of President Washington's mother, Mary Ball Washington, is a short walk from it. The docents know

Above: The home of Fielding and Betty Washington Lewis in Fredericksburg, Virginia, dates to the 1770s and is now known as Kenmore. *Author's collection.*

Right: George Washington's mother lived for many years in Fredericksburg, Virginia. *Author's collection.*

the exact room where George Washington slept on many of his visits to the mansion, and it's a reasonable assumption that he pulled his boots off within that chamber during his overnight stops on the Southern Tour.

Neither Washington nor other contemporaries rarely, if ever, recorded where Major Jackson or the president's servants ate and slept. In most cases, Major Jackson probably stayed in the same quarters with the president. The others were put up in various ways and places. Of course, it was always important for the horses and equipment to be properly attended, and I suspect, in some cases, that members of the staff slept in barns or perhaps even in the baggage wagon. At day's end, the horses were fed and groomed, with hooves and teeth checked and cleaned. Remember, these horses were the engine of the 1791 equivalent to Air Force One.

Just a short drive from Kenmore, Washington's childhood home by the Rappahannock River has been the site of considerable successful archaeological excavation in recent years, and it was in this town where Washington became a Mason at Fredericksburg Masonic Lodge No. 4, which was established in 1752. The lodge is still active, though it meets in a new building—well, a building from 1816.

By Saturday afternoon, everyone in Fredericksburg knew of Washington's presence. A long tribute and dinner took place at city hall beginning at two o'clock with the mayor serving as lead host. As was custom in the larger communities throughout the tour, Fredericksburg's officials prepared a written address honoring the president and his visit. Typically, city fathers prepared a written address for Major Jackson and Washington's review. Major Jackson would then write a response, and both addresses would be read with fanfare at some point before the president's departure.

Proud of one whom the citizens of Fredericksburg considered a native son, the Fredericksburg address gushed, "The inhabitants of Fredericksburg sir! As they can boast the first acquaintance with your virtues claim a peculiar pleasure in testifying to the world your exalted merit and in joining with the rest of America to express their entire approbation of your conduct thro' life which has been so productive of blessings to its citizens." Washington responded, "At all times flattered by the esteem, and grateful for the good wishes of my fellow citizens I am particularly so when to my respect for their public worth is united the endearment of private acquaintance." Amidst this stiff formal language, it is evident that there was genuine mutual admiration between the president and the citizens of Fredericksburg.

Washington left Fredericksburg by six o'clock on Sunday morning. The president would attend several church services during the trip, but usually not on travel days. And the president was an early riser throughout his life; he once advised his teenage step-grandson George Washington Parke Custis: "Rise early, that by habit it may become familiar, agreeable, healthy, and profitable." Washington definitely lived this maxim during the Southern Tour.

But six o'clock in the morning was not too early for a large group of the area's gentlemen to be saddled up and ready to escort the president out of town. Custom and sentiment of the time was that such a great guest as Washington should not only be received properly upon arrival in a community but also must be properly attended upon departure—anything less than a mounted escort out of town was considered rude. Though Washington enjoyed pomp, ceremony and respectful attention, he did not enjoy the considerable dust stirred-up by well-meaning escorts.

On a typical travel day, the entourage departed between five and six o'clock in the morning, later stopping for breakfast. The morning meal came early some days—within the first hour, but occasionally, it was two or three hours until breakfast. On this particular day, the party split in two as it rolled south along or near present-day Virginia Route 2. The president knew this particular countryside, and he, along with Major Jackson and one servant, soon stopped at a General Spotswood's for breakfast, while the rest of the party proceeded another seven to ten miles before breakfasting at Todd's Ordinary, an inn near present-day Villboro. Just north of the Mattaponi River, thirty-five miles or so from Fredericksburg, the travelers reconvened at Kenner's Tavern for the night.

The next morning, a Monday, with Richmond about thirty miles distant, Washington remained at Kenner's for breakfast before moving along for a two o'clock arrival in the Virginia capital, including a stop midway to refresh the horses. Much of Richmond's population of nearly four thousand was aware of the president's arrival. Throngs gathered to observe a cannon salute and hear greetings from Governor Beverley Randolph. That evening, Richmond was aglow as the city put on an "illumination," a tribute featuring candles, torches and tar barrels. From such comes the phrase "to light up the town."

Virginia was the most populated state in 1791, and its most famous native son visited its capital for four days and three nights. This was Washington's last visit to Richmond, but it was a good and thorough stay. The president resided comfortably in a private home and enjoyed dinners hosted by leading citizens, including the governor and mayor. Washington's other activities included a trip on the James River, a visit to the capitol and a special tour of the James River system of canals and locks.

Left: In 1785, the Virginia General Assembly commissioned French sculptor Jean Antoine Houdon to render a statue of Washington. The marble statue was placed in the Virginia capitol in 1796. *Author's collection.*

Below: The Virginia state capitol, design by Thomas Jefferson, was constructed during the years 1785–92. Washington saw it as a brick building in 1791; the white stucco was added in the late 1790s. *Author's collection.*

Washington was a leading proponent of canal systems, thinking them vital to the growth of American commerce and development. Indeed, he was a stock owner in the James River Canal Company thanks to a gift of shares from the Virginia General Assembly in 1785. The gift was in tribute to Washington for his role and service in the Revolution.

Though immensely interested in the workings and success of the James River Canal, Washington viewed his ownership as honorific, and in 1796, he donated his shares to Liberty Hall Academy of Lexington,

The Washington Memorial on the Virginia capitol grounds took eight years to build and was dedicated on Washington's birthday in 1858. *Author's collection.*

Virginia. The value of the shares remains in the endowment of that school, which is known today as Washington and Lee University.

Edward Carrington was Washington's host in Richmond. Carrington had been an officer in the Continental army and a future mayor of Richmond. At the time of the Southern Tour, Carrington—by Washington's appointment—served as both a U.S. marshal and supervisor of the Virginia revenue district, the structure in place to collect federal tax. So the visit allowed Washington to discuss firsthand with Carrington the means to collect the new tax on domestic whiskey; the president was pleased to hear Carrington's opinion that, generally, the people and legislators of Virginia accepted the new tax.

After breakfast in Richmond on Thursday morning, cannons roared as Washington's caravan rolled across the Mayo Bridge spanning the James River. The James River is about 350 miles long; it flows only in Virginia, making it the twelfth-longest river to run in just a single state. The president was escorted all the way to Petersburg by a variety of citizens and militia, including U.S. marshal Carrington. Washington noted that the land looked poor, supporting mostly pine trees, but he was more impressed with the Appomattox River commerce in Petersburg. After a big dinner with many toasts, each punctuated by a cannon blast, Washington took in an assembly in the Blanford section of the city, home of the still surviving Blanford Church, built in 1735. It was a grand night in Petersburg, though fearful of fire, city leaders nixed a full illumination.

It is not certain where Washington and crew slept in Petersburg, but it was a short night. The president had been highly aggravated by the dust and commotion from the large, endless escort of the preceding day. When asked the evening before at what hour he would leave town, the president responded, "I should endeavor to do it before eight o'clock." But Washington and his band packed up and left shortly after five o'clock, riding twelve miles before stopping for breakfast, leaving behind the well-intentioned inconvenience of many dutiful well-wishers. Washington proudly noted his deceitful and surreptitious act in his travel diary. Even George Washington could tell a lie, albeit an understandable one.

The lightly populated section south of Petersburg was unfamiliar to Washington. Following roads that roughly trace today's U.S. 301 and Interstate 95, the group entered an area where stages for food and lodging were farther apart and generally of poor quality. The president was pleased with the House of Oliver, somewhere near present-day south central Sussex County, as he said it was a good stop for the horses.

President Washington was probably entertained at the Golden Ball Tavern in the heart of Petersburg, Virginia. *Author's collection.*

The Petersburg, Virginia courthouse, built during 1838–40, is one of the most distinctive and handsome buildings in town. *Author's collection.*

On Saturday, April 16, the travelers set out at five o'clock in the morning and endured violent, stormy weather most of the day. The spring and summer of 1791 were exceedingly dry in the region, and Mount Vernon's crops suffered a drought that year. But torrential rain fell that day, so much so that even the rugged George Washington was ready to halt for the day, but finding no suitable lodging for man or horse, the group pressed all the way to Halifax, North Carolina, traveling forty-eight miles. It was perhaps the highest-mileage day of the Southern Tour, and it culminated with George Washington in position for his first true visit to North Carolina.

Chapter 5

THROUGH THE CAROLINAS' COASTAL PLAIN TO CHARLESTON

G iven the storms and downpours, Washington had to be relieved to cross the Roanoke River to Halifax, a fairly bustling center of commerce and the home of a few men of statewide prominence. In colonial days, the state legislature often met in Halifax, and it was here in April 1776 that representatives of the colony gathered to put forth the Halifax Resolves, which called for North Carolina, and indeed all of the colonies, to gain their independence from Great Britain.

Events in colonial Halifax may have been a precursor to Philadelphia and the Declaration of Independence in July 1776, but upon his arrival in Carolina nearly fifteen years later, Washington and crew were just hoping to get themselves and the horses out of the weather. Washington's journal entry spoke of a day that began in a cloud of dust as the caravan rolled forth at five o'clock in the morning but shortly thereafter turned to rain and storms. Noting the flat terrain of tidewater Virginia and coastal Carolina, the president wrote, "My passage was through water; so level are the roads."

One of Halifax's prominent men was Willie Jones, North Carolina's anti-Federalist leader, whom Benjamin Hawkins mentioned in his recent letter to the president. Jones was important enough in Halifax that, undoubtedly, it lessened the show of enthusiasm from Washington's strongest supporters. However, Washington was received by North Carolina congressman John Baptista Ashe, who was on hand for the president's two-night stay that included a dinner with area leaders and visits with local Masonic brethren,

The William R. Davie home in Halifax, North Carolina, was built in the 1780s. Davie was among the state's foremost leaders of the late eighteenth century and is considered the founder of the University of North Carolina. *Author's collection.*

It's not known if Washington lodged at Eagle Tavern during his two-night stay in Halifax, North Carolina. *Author's collection.*

members of one of the Tar Heel State's oldest lodges. It is not clear how much interaction took place between Washington and Jones.

Today, the State of North Carolina preserves and operates a portion of the old town that Washington visited. Historic Halifax is a state historic site adjacent to a very small ongoing real Halifax that still serves as the county seat of Halifax County. The nearby Roanoke River sees little commerce these days; it's mostly recreational.

To catch a glimpse of the river on a weekend visit to Halifax, I drove down a road posted "Halifax Fishing Club, Members Only." As one who typically obeys rules, regulations and signs, this was, for me, a walk on the wild side. As the river came into view, I took note of a number of small shacks and buildings between the road and river, which I took to be fishing huts. There was no way to see the brown waters of the Roanoke very well without approaching some of the huts.

When I spied four men on an open porch facing the river, I decided to introduce myself and try to make new friends while averting a trespassing charge. The men were spending their Saturday doing a little fishing, a little beer drinking and a lot of talking. Friendly enough, they offered me a brew and a chair on the porch around a table topped with the latest *Playboy* and a variety of sports and fishing magazines.

I told them about my interest in George Washington's visit to Halifax; this immediately led to jokes about how several of them were old enough to recall that occasion. Smiling but moving past their amusement, I told them about the Southern Tour. My companions did not really know or care much about my historical interests, but they kindly listened, and I enjoyed their company. They answered some questions about how deep the river was and told me how one could easily take shallow-draft boats up the river seven miles to Weldon, and they spoke about things down river where it dumps into the Albemarle Sound.

During the forty-minute visit, cardinals, bluebirds, goldfinches and Carolina chickadees flitted about, and I asked about the fish that I saw frequently jumping in mid-river channel. "Jumping mullets!" they all exclaimed. "Those are jumping mullets!" Like George Washington, I met some new people in Halifax, and perhaps, I saw something that he didn't—jumping mullets.

On Monday and Tuesday, April 18 and 19, Washington's progression took him to Tarboro, where he indicated that he received as good a salute as possible with a single piece of artillery; Greenville, where he observed tar in production; and an overnight stay with Shadrach Allen near present-day Ayden, which today is a small burg known for its pork barbecue. In Tarboro, despite its limited artillery, Washington was impressed with a bridge—rare structures at the time—that carried travelers over the Tar River.

At Shadrach Allen's, the president groused that it was a very indifferent house, and he was concerned that the horses had to stand without cover for the first time on the trip. But after all, it was the evening of April 19, well into spring, and horses often went without a stable this far south. It is worth noting that Washington generally used *indifferent* to convey a stronger negative connotation than the present-day understanding of the word, which implies that something is mediocre. But certainly, Washington, an exacting man, was no fan of things indifferent, whether it meant mediocre or poor.

Washington learned about the prominence of tobacco in this section of North Carolina and how it was rolled to market in hogsheads, essentially a big rolling barrel pulled by a horse. And he saw some of the chief commerce of the state, naval stores, involving the production of timber, tar, pitch and turpentine for shipbuilding and ship maintenance. North Carolina was a world leader in tar production from the late 1700s through the nineteenth century.

In the first half of the twentieth century, the North Carolina Daughters of the American Revolution marked many Southern Tour stops in the state, including this one on the grounds of the Pitt County courthouse in Greenville. *Author's collection.*

After the night at Shadrach Allen's, the entourage traveled a short distance and then breakfasted with another Mr. Allen, probably Shadrach's brother, John. Though the guests were unexpected, Allen and his wife were well aware of the prominence of the travelers and wanted to offer a large and varied breakfast. Mrs. Allen relished the task and, eventually, prepared a groaning board filled with typical southern fare derived from pork, poultry and corn.

Despite the feast before him, the legend goes that the Allens were disappointed when Washington asked just for a boiled egg and coffee with a shot of rum. It was only when the president asked for a bill that he discovered that he was in a private home, not an inn; Mr. Allen refused to accept payment from Washington. Now embarrassed, the president awkwardly gave Mrs. Allen a quick kiss for her trouble—perhaps that morning's visit can be called the "buss" stop. In this instance, Washington had unwittingly violated his own rule of not accepting personal hospitality.

An additional tale from this stop is that a pretty young woman joined the president in his chariot as it departed from this breakfast stop, but no scandalous aspect accompanies the story. Some local historians offer that the attractive rider was probably the Allens' daughter

In April 2015, a reenactor portrayed President Washington's arrival in New Bern, North Carolina, during that city's weekend-long commemoration of the Southern Tour. *Author's collection.*

catching a ride to New Bern, an understandable accommodation the president might allow considering the confusion during his visit.

About ten miles from New Bern, then the largest town in North Carolina, a group of locals greeted Washington and led the way to the town of 2,500 established in 1710 at the convergence of the Neuse and Trent Rivers. Here, Washington would spend two nights—probably staying in a stellar example of Georgian architecture, the John Wright Stanly home, today a tourist attraction.

New Bern's weather, natural beauty, charm, history and surrounding waters make it a popular destination for retirees and tourists. Carbonated drinks have a big legacy in the South; it was in 1896 that a New Bern pharmacist concocted Pepsi-Cola. Much older than Pepsi's creation are some ancient trees in town, especially a one-thousand-year-old bald cypress behind the Smallwood House on Front Street. Washington saw the tree on his visit. The bald cypress has few enemies in the form of disease and insects and has a high wind resistance. Survivors of innumerable hurricanes, ancient specimens dot the coastal regions of the South.

On the second of two nights in New Bern, Washington was treated to a festive public dinner and dance at the Tryon Palace, the once grand colonial

The president's dance card was full during a ball held in his honor at Tryon Palace in New Bern, North Carolina. *Author's collection.*

governors' seat of government. Washington, always a man of details, noted that about seventy ladies were at the dance and that New Bern was about seventy miles from the sea by water but much closer by land.

Toasts were an important part of the many dinners honoring Washington. Typically, there would be at least thirteen toasts, a form of arithmetic to honor each of the states. At New Bern's festive occasion, the crowd raised their glasses fifteen times in tribute to:

- the United States
- the late Congress
- the State of North Carolina (given by the president)
- the patriots of America who fell in its defense
- the late American army
- the king of France
- the National Assembly
- the memory of Dr. Franklin
- the Sieur de la Fayette
- the commerce of the United States
- the friends of America in every part of the world
- the agricultural interests of the United States
- the nations in alliance with us
- universal peace and liberty

And finally, with all present standing:

To the president of the United States. Huzzah! Huzzah! Huzzah!

New Bern's big dinner and dance kept the president engaged from midafternoon until he retired at eleven o'clock, though the dance and social continued well past his departure. The following morning, New Bern's leadership, or as Washington called them, the "principal gentlemen of New Bern," escorted the president's group south toward the wilds of Jones County, a rustic, poor and lightly populated county named in honor of none other than Willie Jones. In North Carolina, both Washington and his nemesis Jones were living legends and had places named in their honor.

For better or worse, the escort from New Bern soon dropped off, leaving the travelers in rugged but flat and low country, maybe fifty feet above sea level, on poorly marked roads. The group took a meal in Trenton and lodged at Shine's Tavern, despite its remote and rural location one of the better, more reliable inns in eastern Carolina.

On the morning of Saturday, April 23, more than two weeks since leaving Mount Vernon but still a good 250 miles from Charleston, the president and his retinue were entering a desolate stretch, unescorted over rough and poorly marked roads, at first through a vast longleaf pine forest and then along South Carolina's Atlantic Coast. Except for Wilmington, North Carolina, and Georgetown, South Carolina, the source of food, shelter and provisions for man and horse were uncertain between there and Charleston.

Washington had never seen such a vast longleaf pine savanna as he witnessed during his passage through southeastern North Carolina. The foundation of naval store commerce, longleaf pines supplied timber and the makings of tar, pitch and turpentine. As the caravan bounced toward Wilmington surrounded by endless tall pines with little underbrush save wire grass, the president wrote, "The whole road passes through the most barren country I ever beheld." Though Washington was disappointed by the prospective use of this land for agriculture, he did see beauty in it. He wrote, "The appearances of it are agreeable, resembling a lawn well covered with evergreens and a good verdure below from a broom or course grass…there were parts entirely open and others with ponds of water which contributed not a little to the beauty of the scene."

When European settlement began, the longleaf pine, relatively rare now, covered over half the land in the coastal states from Virginia to Texas. Today, according to Lawrence Earley in his book *Looking for Longleaf*, the once abundant tree covers less than 1.5 percent of the land in those states. Some scientists think that restoration of longleaf pine forests might counteract global warming, and their renewal is being advanced by foresters. But early travelers complained that the forests were so vast and unchanging that the traveler could hardly sense if he were moving at all. The two days in the longleaf savanna made an impression on George Washington, a lifelong outdoorsman.

In addition to the large cypress and longleaf pine trees, as Washington moved farther south, he likely saw some of his favorite blooms—those of the redbud tree and dogwood tree. Redbud and dogwood are still abundant in the South, but since Washington's day, there are many imported newcomers, like crape myrtles, which were just beginning to arrive in America from Asia in the 1790s.

Japanese honeysuckle arrived in the States in the early nineteenth century. This invasive non-native can be a pesky vine, but its sweet aroma

The Carolina parakeet, the only native parrot to North America, once ranged over much of the eastern United States but was especially abundant in the South. The last two Carolina parakeets in captivity died in the Cincinnati Zoo in the late 1910s. *Courtesy of the North Carolina Collection–Chapel Hill.*

is a delight to most spring travelers who open a window or sunroof. By May, the fragrance of honeysuckle pervades the air in the Piedmont and the Coastal Plain of North Carolina. Alas, though I know and enjoy the imported honeysuckle and crape myrtle, Washington's travelers took note of native birds that I have never seen—passenger pigeons and Carolina parakeets. Those birds are now extinct. I find the loss of the colorful parakeet especially sad; it was the only parakeet native to the land that became the United States.

Washington and Major Jackson certainly carried maps covering the route of the tour. The president was quite familiar with the roads and water crossings between Philadelphia and Richmond, but the land and roads south of the James were unfamiliar. Based on Washington's maps, found today in collections at Yale University and the American Geographical Society, the president presumably packed several maps in his trunk or valise covering the South, among them *A Map of the Inhabited Part of Virginia*, made by Fry and Jefferson in 1775; *John Collet's 1770 Map of North Carolina, An Accurate Map of North and South Carolina*, made by Mouzon in 1775; and a *Map of South Carolina and Part of Georgia*, made by DeBrahm, dating to 1757.

The maps—along with the notes and suggestions that Washington and his secretaries gathered on roads, mileages and inns—helped guide these high-ranking tourists. Though the cavalcade was often escorted by local leaders and militia, I suspect that Washington and Jackson often referred to the maps to get their bearings and to satisfy their curiosity. After all, there is some satisfaction in seeing on a map where you have been as well as where you are going, plus these former army officers were accustomed to maps and their usage.

On April 22 and 23, the travelers surely referred to all navigational resources and instincts as they made their way unescorted through the lightly populated forest toward a connection with the King's Highway. After spending a night near present-day Holly Ridge, Washington awoke on Easter Sunday bound for Wilmington. Holly Ridge, just a few miles from Topsail Beach and the Atlantic Ocean, is a quiet crossroads these days, as it has been for much of the past two hundred years, but for a short few years in the early 1940s, its nickname was "Boomtown."

Holly Ridge, along U.S. 17, bustled and boomed for a few brief years during World War II as the home of Camp Davis, a temporary anti-aircraft training camp. At one point in 1943, 110,000 troops were stationed in Holly Ridge, served by one thousand temporary buildings and miles and miles of paved roads and airstrips on over ten thousand acres. U.S. 17—the King's Highway in Washington's day—and the Atlantic Coast Line Railroad linked the isolated camp to the world.

At war's end, Camp Davis was decommissioned and deconstructed, leaving the asphalt roads and airstrips as telltale signs that something big was once there. The camp's supporting businesses in Holly Ridge, with the loss of the bulk of their clientele, disappeared in short order. Gone, too, was the nightlife of Holly Ridge, the restaurants and bars, such as the Bucket O' Blood Saloon.

Except for occasional busy periods in beach-going season, Holly Ridge—about midway between Camp Lejeune Marine Base and Wilmington—has mostly been a place of calm and quiet through its history. Just over 150 years after Washington's passage, Holly Ridge's brief boom went bust. In recent years, Camp Lejeune Marine Base has taken over a fair share of the lands of the old Camp Davis, including many of the old roads.

As Washington pushed on to Wilmington, he had yet to glimpse the Atlantic Ocean, which was just a few miles to the east, and the entourage was probably unaware of being in the midst of several other rare forms of nature: the Venus' flytrap, eastern coral snakes and peat bogs.

Though the insect-consuming flytrap grows well in many places around the world, the plant is native only to an area, say, fifty miles from Wilmington. The number of flytraps has been in a long decline, and both it and the longleaf pine have a reseeding process that thrives on fire. So, ironically, man's control of fire is among factors leading to the loss of longleaf and the flytrap. The Venus' flytrap is protected by law in North Carolina, and poachers can be prosecuted.

The northern range of the eastern coral snake, a slim, venomous snake adorned in red, yellow and black bands, begins along the coastal area north of Wilmington and persists along the Atlantic Coast all the way down through South Carolina, Georgia and Florida and then continues along all of the Gulf Coast. At a glance, it is difficult to distinguish between the coral snake and the harmless king snake, which is very similar in appearance. The important distinction is in the arrangement of their colorful bands. In coral snakes, the red and yellow bands are adjacent. Hence the rhyme: Red and Yellow, Hurt a Fellow—Red and Black, A Friend of Jack. Washington, at ease in nature, surely saw many snakes in his day, but he made no reference to reptiles in his diary during this trip.

Washington, ever the farmer, regularly took note of the soil. Perhaps he saw mostly sandy soil along his coastal passage on the King's Highway, but near his route were swamps and organic soil. The rich, organic soil, or peat, can burn six to ten feet below the surface and can be a nightmare for firefighters. In general, the makeup of organic soil varies widely, and some is

This ancient sprawling live oak tree is on the shoulder of U.S. 17, formerly the King's Highway. Legend goes that Washington's entourage stopped here for a break on Easter Sunday in 1791. *Courtesy of Beth Boney Jenkins.*

much more agriculturally productive than others. Just west of Washington's route between Holly Ridge and Wilmington is the Holly Shelter Swamp and Game Land, a superb place to take in nature, both flora and fauna.

As the entourage came within twelve miles of Wilmington, it was met by an escort of Wilmington militia and gentlemen. The entire group entered town in a processional; the president likely mounted Prescott and rode into Wilmington under cannon salute around two o'clock in the afternoon. John Huske of Wilmington, a noted anti-Federalist, led the cannon tribute. Despite his negative sentiment toward the government led by President Washington, apparently, Huske had no trouble calling the volleys.

Though it was Easter, Washington did not attend a church service. After several days of "indifferent" food and lodging, he was pleased to be in Wilmington, where he stayed in the home of a prominent widow, Mrs. John Quince, at the corner of Front and Dock Streets. Nothing scandalous was at hand; the widow stayed with relatives during the president's visit.

Among Wilmington's population of one thousand or so were a number of Freemasons, who were surely front and center as Washington's hosts. The first Masonic lodge in North Carolina was established in Wilmington in 1754. The community dinner for Washington shortly after his arrival was held at Dorsey's Tavern, owned and operated by a Mason, Lawrence Dorsey. Many prominent early Americans were Masons, and foremost among them was the nation's first president. Certainly, Brother Dorsey was proud to receive Washington, American hero and fellow Mason.

The Cape Fear River was easily navigable for larger vessels from its mouth to Wilmington, which made the small city North Carolina's chief port. So Wilmington was an active place at the junction of the King's Highway and the Cape Fear River. By the time of Washington's visit, a stagecoach had begun operation along the coast of North Carolina—from Edenton to Washington to Wilmington. Today, Wilmington is at one end of Interstate 40, which traverses the United States, exactly 2,554 miles from Barstow, California—every mile of it is limited access multi-lane paved asphalt. Such remarkable roads that we take for granted were George Washington's science fiction.

Wilmington provided a nice reception for Washington. In addition to the opening parade and cannon tribute, colorful banners hung from buildings and ships, bonfires and illuminations of various sort brightened the nights and the president was treated to two community dinners and a dance. Widow Quince's home made for "very good lodgings." Secretary William Jackson kept busy with correspondence, answering the address from the citizens of Wilmington as well as a letter from Charles Pinckney of Charleston. Additionally, Jackson drafted for Washington's signature a letter of appointment to a William Cooke of Wilmington, who Washington offered command of the area's U.S. revenue cutter.

North Carolina did not settle on a permanent capital until 1792, when Raleigh was established by the legislature and laid out in the woods of rural Wake County. Over the years, the legislature met in different places—among them Halifax, Tarboro, Hillsborough and New Bern—and had most recently met frequently in Fayetteville. After two nights in Wilmington, a representative from Fayetteville traveling by horse caught up with Washington in Brunswick County, south of Wilmington, to bring written greetings from officials of the occasional capital of the state.

In essence, at the time of Washington's visit, North Carolina did not have a permanent capital, making it the only state of the Southern Tour in which the president did not visit its seat of government. William Jackson quickly penned a reply to the citizens of Fayetteville in which Washington thanked them for their attention and affections. As Washington signed that letter, he surely thought of his dear French friend from the Revolution, the Marquis de Lafayette, for whom Fayetteville was named.

An escort from Wilmington led Washington south along the King's Highway for part of Tuesday, the twenty-sixth, but once again, the entourage was soon on its own in a rugged coastal region, present-day Brunswick County. Helen Turner descends from a long-established family there; she told me that Washington crossed Town Creek on her family's land but did not know much else about where he passed in her native county.

There were apparently few, if any, decent inns between Wilmington and Georgetown. The men and horses pressed on and made do. The so-called inns in this remote stretch benefitted from the "any port in a storm" syndrome; they mostly were ramshackle homes where the owner took in overnighters for a fee.

Boundary House, a form of rest stop and inn, was a long-running concern operating atop the Carolinas boundary line near the Atlantic Ocean. The house was in place by 1754 and was active into the nineteenth century. Back in mid-April before Washington's arrival in the region, a prominent visitor there worried that Boundary House was ill-prepared to host the president as it had no flour and rum was its only liquor. There is no evidence that Washington stopped there, but the presidential group did know of it and probably considered it.

The entourage entered South Carolina just above present-day Little River shortly after noon on April 27, finishing the day about sixteen miles into the Palmetto State, just a couple of miles shy of what was then known as Long Bay. Today, Long Bay is known as Myrtle Beach. Washington and crew spent a night there before tackling Long Bay the next morning.

In this section of South Carolina, travelers in Washington's time often used local guides to direct them across inlets at low tide, thus allowing a much more direct route than allowed by staying on the north–south roads farther inland. Jeremiah Vareen Jr. piloted the president's cavalcade across the swash. Washington wrote, "Mr. Vareen piloted us across the Swash (which at high water is impassable, and at times, by the shifting of the sands is dangerous) on to the long Beach of the Ocean; and it being at a proper time of the tide we passed along it with ease and celerity to the place of quitting it which is estimated 16 miles."

Washington's caravan rode the length of an undeveloped and quiet Myrtle Beach at low tide! What a remarkable image, especially knowing the beach today as a place of traffic congestion, high-rise buildings, tacky amusements, golf courses, beach homes and high density of various commercial and residential buildings.

A few miles after Long Bay, the travelers took a break at George Pawley's, feeding themselves and the horses. Pawley was likely of the same family for which nearby Pawley's Island is named. Pawley's, a proud, small island of charming—but not necessarily fancy—old homes goes by the motto, "Arrogantly Shabby" and is known for producing Pawley's Island hammocks, enduring, handmade rope hammocks. After their rest, the travelers went another ten miles before finding an evening sanctuary at Brookgreen Plantation. Today's Brookgreen Gardens, accessible from U.S. 17, is a vestige of the plantation. For the day, Washington's odometer recorded thirty-three miles. With inlet crossings and beach roadways, it was a different sort of day—and probably an enjoyable one.

The following morning, as Washington continued south for a breakfast stop, the entourage was met by an escort of three gentlemen from Charleston, William Moultrie, William Washington and John Rutledge Jr. Moultrie was a hero of the Revolution in South Carolina, and William Washington, who also had enjoyed a distinguished military career, was the president's cousin who had married into an affluent South Carolina family. John Rutledge Jr. was the son of Justice Rutledge, who was distinguished and sat on both the U.S. and South Carolina Supreme Courts.

Washington was moving into rice country, and by now, the semi-tropical vegetation was dense. The icon of South Carolina, the cabbage palmetto tree, was abundant by the road, as were sprawling evergreen live oaks draped

Washington was entertained at the Stewart-Parker House in Georgetown, South Carolina. Alongside the Sampit River, the home, built in the mid-1700s, is owned by Colonial Dames of South Carolina and open for tours. *Author's collection.*

in Spanish moss. The president was in a different land; perhaps only on his teenage trip to Barbados had he seen any place quite like it.

Arriving in Georgetown on Saturday, the thirtieth, Washington had to be pleased with the reception given by the town he reckoned to be no larger than five or six hundred in population. Washington entered town by water and was rowed across the Waccamaw River by specially uniformed sea captains, and upon arrival, he was treated to a cannon salute, addresses by the town officials and the Masons, a tea party with the ladies and a public dinner and dance. Washington gushed in his diary that "upwards of 50 ladies assembled for the tea party and that rice was the place's chief export." Washington failed to note in his journal that on that date two years earlier—April 30—he had been inaugurated president. Perhaps he was too consumed with the trip for the anniversary to have crossed his mind.

Georgetown has a fascinating history. Today, it is a tourist hub and a place of industry along its rivers, but the first Methodist church in South Carolina was established in Georgetown in 1785 by Bishop Francis Asbury, though Anglican and even Jewish worshippers gathered there much earlier. The Winyah Indigo Society, established around 1740 as a social society for planters, still exists but now accepts members other than planters. The Rice Museum is a popular attraction in downtown Georgetown. Until the mid-1850s, South Carolina produced the majority of American-grown rice.

On Sunday, May 1, the group hit the trail—or, in this case, the water—at six o'clock in the morning when the same sea captains who had brought them in rowed the group south across the Sampit River. All of Georgetown was awake, if for no other reason than because the artillery once again roared as the president crossed the river. Washington was invited to an elegant reception and brunch at Hampton Plantation, perhaps the state's largest rice producer. Pieces of the green and white Wedgewood china used at Hampton that special day are on display at the Charleston Museum. The travelers ended their day as private guests of Joseph Manigault of Awendaw Plantation; the one place that Washington was determined to visit on the Southern Tour was just ahead—Charleston.

While the entourage moved through Lowcountry South Carolina, presidential secretary Tobias Lear wrote the president from Philadelphia on May 1 to advise that Mrs. Washington had decided to visit friends in Jersey for a few days. With Lear's assistance, a coach and four horses and a driver were procured at a cost of twenty-four dollars, "cheaper than Mrs.

The Hampton Plantation mansion dates to the 1730s and was owned by the Horry and Rutledge families for over two hundred years. Today, it's a South Carolina State Historic Site. Washington took a midday meal here on May 1, 1791. *Author's collection.*

When Hampton Plantation matron Eliza Lucas Pinckney advised Washington that she planned to cut down the live oak tree growing close to the house, the president discouraged the tree's removal. The massive tree is now around 250 years old. *Author's collection.*

Upon departure from Hampton Plantation, the Southern Tour entourage soon passed Saint James Santee Church (or Wambaw Church). Built circa 1768, the church is alongside a stretch of the original unpaved King's Highway. *Author's collection.*

Washington could go in her own coach." Matters of government were pretty quiet, as most of Lear's letter addressed household concerns.

By midafternoon the next day, May 2, the men covered the twenty-five miles or so to Haddrell's Point across from Charleston on the Cooper River. That's when the festivities began. The river and Charleston Harbor were full of decorated boats, cannons roared and musicians filled several boats—instruments were played and choirs sang:

> *He Comes! He comes! The hero comes.*
> *Sound, sound your trumpets, beat your drums.*
> *From port to port let cannons roar,*
> *His welcome to our friendly shore.*

Charleston wanted to impress the president, and the president wanted to impress Charleston. The gentlemen of coastal South Carolina were largely supporters of the Constitution and Federalism, and Washington knew he needed their leadership in the South. The president, still often called "General Washington," took his commander in chief role seriously and probably wore his uniform and sword that day, perhaps for the first time on the trip.

Thirteen sea captains in light blue silk jackets, one to represent each state of the Union, rowed Washington across the Cooper on a barge, not too far from where today's travelers cross the river on the long, sweeping, modern Arthur J. Ravenel Jr. Bridge. The hosts, including South Carolina governor Charles Pinckney, led Washington straight to the Exchange Building at the foot of Broad Street, where a parade ensued for the president's review. Charleston's dirt and sand streets had been swept and watered for the occasion.

Washington was pleased when he saw his fancy lodgings on Church Street, the townhome of planter Thomas Heyward Jr. The city rented Heyward's home for Washington and even staffed it. After three and a half weeks of hustle and bustle since leaving Mount Vernon, the entourage found itself in Charleston for a week, a welcome change of pace for all the travelers—man and beast.

While in Charleston, Washington was heavily scheduled—yet he enjoyed some spare time to simply ride horseback and look around the city. He was surely pleased with trips across Charleston Harbor to visit the Revolutionary War sites of Fort Moultrie on Sullivan's Island and Fort Johnson on James Island. Fort Moultrie's fame dates to its successful defense of Charleston against the British in 1776. British cannonballs seemingly bounced off the little fort of Palmetto logs.

The fort was generally in continuous service through World War II and today is Fort Moultrie National Monument, where visitors not only learn the history of the fort but also can enjoy great views across the water of Charleston's skyline and of Fort Sumter, a site of Civil War fame. Among the many soldiers stationed at Fort Moultrie throughout its history were writer Edgar Allan Poe, who as an enlisted man who served there in 1827–28, and the great George C. Marshall, the World War II and early Cold War leader, who served at Moultrie in 1933.

Washington was wined and dined daily in Charleston. In a way, it must have been as tedious as the uncertain, long days traveling through the longleaf pines. But Washington thrived in pomp, ceremony, good food and entertainment. He knew he had to act his role and appear to enjoy it; the citizenry deserved nothing less.

He was regaled and hosted by Masons, the Society of the Cincinnati, local and state civic leaders and the ladies of the community. One night, the president was saluted by ship-borne fireworks, and on the consecutive

Washington attended a concert at the Exchange Building in Charleston, South Carolina, with "at least 400 ladies whose number and appearances exceeded anything of the kind he had ever seen." *Author's collection.*

evenings of May 4 and 5, Washington's journal entries gushed about the "elegantly dressed and handsome ladies of Charleston" who attended a concert and dancing assembly in numbers of 256 and at least 400, "their number and appearances exceeded anything of the kind the president had ever seen." The love affair was mutual. One evening, a banner hung from the still extant Exchange Building. It read, "With grateful praises of the hero's fame, we'll teach our infants' tongues to lisp his name."

For the entire trip, Washington's diary never alludes to practical matters of comfort stops and washing clothes, but comfort and clean clothes were surely a welcome part of the stay in Charleston. Even the staff and horses had time to clean up and rest, though they were busy attending to the president's needs, too, while he went from engagement to engagement. The Charleston stop was likely a fond memory for all of the travelers. Months after the conclusion of the Southern Tour, Washington even exchanged letters with the woman who served as lead attendant of his guest quarters.

William Jackson probably joined the president at most of his Charleston engagements, but he had his ongoing secretarial duties penning addresses to Charleston's city officials, merchants and Masons and assisting the president with letters on May 7 and 8, including short missives to Alexander Hamilton and Thomas Jefferson and a longer letter to the commissioners of the federal city, where Washington worried that area landowners—despite his favorable meetings with them in April—would let their personal interests or greed stand in the way of making their land available for a national capital.

On Sunday, May 8, Washington spent his last day in Charleston, and he treated it as the Sabbath—unscheduled, except for two church services when he attended two Episcopal churches, St. Philip's in the morning and St. Michael's in the afternoon. At this point in his life, Washington rarely took communion, perhaps partly because he eschewed the more public prospect of parading to the altar, but you can bet that everyone knew that day that George Washington, one of the most famous persons in the world, was in their midst.

To commemorate Washington's visit, Charleston's city council soon commissioned John Trumbull to paint a portrait of Washington. Trumbull was an accomplished artist and was already quite familiar with Washington; he had painted Washington's likeness several times and had served the general as an aide during the Revolution.

Trumbull treated the Charleston commission quite seriously and worked diligently toward a special portrait depicting a heroic Washington standing alongside his tall white horse at Trenton during the Revolution. However, Charleston's city fathers rejected the painting, desiring instead a portrait featuring an older, present-day Washington along with some visual elements specific to his visit to Charleston.

Once again, Trumbull painted a uniformed Washington by his white horse, but this time, he portrayed the fifty-nine-year-old Washington with

The cornerstone of Saint Michael's Church in Charleston was laid in 1752. During the Southern Tour, Washington worshipped here and enjoyed a view of the city by climbing the steeple to the lantern level. The author followed in Washington's footsteps by making the same climb. *Author's collection.*

the Charleston skyline in the background. The Charleston painting hangs in city hall as part of a notable portrait gallery. The Charleston City Hall Gallery is open to the public, and visitors can't miss Washington's portrait: it is huge and placed front and center. Trumbull's first effort for his Charleston commission hangs in the Yale Art Gallery far to the north along the Atlantic Coast in Trumbull's home state of Connecticut. The two portraits, displayed nearly nine hundred miles apart, are each vestiges of George Washington's Southern Tour.

By six o'clock in the morning on Monday, May 9, Washington's and his escorts were heading south from Charleston. The president had on clean clothes, and his boots and ego had been buffed to a shine.

Top: President Washington sat in Saint Michael's pew number forty-three for services on May 8, 1791. *Author's collection.*

Right: In 1791, the City of Charleston commissioned portrait artist John Trumbull to paint this portrait to commemorate Washington's visit to their city. The portrait hangs in the Charleston City Hall art gallery. *Courtesy of the City of Charleston.*

Chapter 6

ONWARD TO SAVANNAH AND AUGUSTA

Though Charleston was the key place for the president to visit, a representative visit to all southern states was important, and Georgia was still ahead. Today, Georgia is a large state in area, nearly sixty thousand square miles, but in 1791, most of present-day Georgia was designated Indian Territory, reserved for elements of the Creek and Cherokee tribes. Georgia was not very large in 1791, and its principal cities were Savannah and Augusta. The entourage's next target was Savannah.

Washington made connections with family members throughout the trip. Back in Virginia, there was tea with his niece in Dumfries and an overnight with his sister Bettie Lewis in Fredericksburg. Now as the president plowed through Lowcountry South Carolina with Georgia on his mind, his first overnight stop was twenty-eight miles distant at his cousin William Washington's, the squire of Sandy Hill Plantation. William Washington was a native Virginian who distinguished himself as a cavalry officer in the Carolinas during the Revolution. After the war, he married South Carolinian Jane Elliott, whose dowry included Sandy Hill. Similar to his cousin George, William Washington found a mate who brought both emotional and fiscal assets to the marriage.

Among many agricultural pursuits, William Washington bred horses. Apparently during this short visit, the cousins talked specifically about mules. George Washington was breeding mules back at Mount Vernon, mostly with some donkeys sent from Europe as gifts, including one from the king of Spain. Washington dubbed that jackass Royal Gift. Some months after this visit, Washington sent Royal Gift overland to Cousin William in South Carolina. Sadly, Royal Gift was unable to perform and was returned by sea to Mount Vernon, where he lived out his days forever infertile.

Washington's route to Savannah was a winding, twisting maze, but he was escorted all the way by some of his Charleston gentlemen friends, spending each night in a private home. There were few, if any, decent public houses in this land of sprawling plantations.

Near Washington's route is present-day Walterboro, a charming old town with tabby sidewalks; tabby pavement is created by mixing crushed oyster shells with sand and lime. The main street is named Washington in honor of George, and not far off it is the South Carolina Artisans Center, which promotes Lowcountry arts and crafts. This area not only promotes its arts but also its history. A few years ago, the local historical society of Colleton County spent a Saturday in May following Washington's path through the county by a horse-drawn coach. That Coaching Day event got a good deal of media coverage around the state, reminding South Carolinians that, yes, George Washington did indeed sleep there.

By Thursday, May 12, the entourage was closing in on Georgia, but it would be a long day. The group was on the road by five o'clock in the

Eerie, haunting, charming, romantic and beautiful are words used to describe the ruins of Old Sheldon Church near Yemasee, South Carolina. Washington passed near here on the way to Savannah, Georgia. *Author's collection.*

morning, first traveling twenty-two miles to Purrysburg, South Carolina, on the Savannah River. After a meal in Purrysburg, the group boarded boats provided by an escort from Savannah. Among the boats was one expressly for Washington, an eight-oared barge rowed by sea captains. But the captains found the wind and tide were against them most of the way down to Savannah.

The hardworking rowers did catch some rest along the way at Mulberry Grove Plantation, the late Nathanael Greene's seat on the Georgia side of the river. Greene, the commanding general and hero of the Southern Department of the Revolution, had been given the land as a reward for his heroic service by the State of Georgia. Sadly, Greene died of sunstroke back in 1786, but his wife kept things going at Mulberry.

Washington knew Greene's widow, Catherine, and he wanted to stop and pay his respects. At Mulberry, the travelers left the flotilla, opting to go overland the last twelve miles to Savannah. Washington groused that the normal four-hour trip from Purrysburg to Savannah had taken seven hours, but his spirits were renewed by a large gathering of greeters in Savannah. At dark, the city was aglow in every way. A general illumination of Savannah was struck to honor the president. Candles, torches and tar barrels lit up the little city on the Georgia coast.

After his visit, President Washington donated these cannons to the City of Savannah in tribute to their notable American Revolutionary War unit, the Chatham Artillery. Residents playfully refer to the cannons as "George" and "Martha." *Author's collection.*

This stone building along the Savannah River is one of the few surviving eighteenth-century buildings in Savannah, Georgia. *Author's collection.*

The Pirate's House is a Savannah restaurant housed in an eighteenth-century building. *Author's collection.*

The president likely slept well his first night in Savannah; he had good lodgings at the end of a long day. The aging commander would have slept even better had he known that Thomas Jefferson had written him back on May 8, "The last week does not furnish one single public event worthy communicating to you: so I have only to say all is well." Washington spent Friday, Saturday and part of Sunday, May 13 through 15, in Savannah and, blessedly, suffered no ill fortune on that Friday, the thirteenth.

Washington visited sites from Revolutionary War battles, considered the waterfront commerce and was fêted roundly by the usual cast of civic and military leaders. After services at Christ Church on Sunday morning, the oldest church in Georgia, the president turned northwest toward Augusta, at that time the capital. After the Sunday church service, Washington was probably both honored and bothered by the presence of several militia members from Augusta who were at the ready to escort the president to their town.

Recipe for Chatham Artillery Punch

This loaded beverage lives up to the name punch, and those who imbibe it are led to overuse corny puns about "having a blast." Created in Savannah in the mid-nineteenth century, the punch remains a popular liquid tribute to the long-standing Chatham Artillery of Savannah, the oldest military unit in the Peach State. Some Savannahians are proud of the heritage and potency of this concoction, which lore says was actually developed by members of the Chatham Artillery. Supporters claim the punch tastes great and is more powerful than any cannon ever fired. Upon Washington's arrival in Savannah on May 12, 1791, Chatham Artillery offered a cannon salute and joined a processional that led the president to his quarters at St. James Square, now Telfair Square.

A recipe for two and a half gallons:

3 pints of Catawba wine
1 pint of rum
1 pint of gin
1 pint of brandy
½ pint of Benedictine
1 pint of Maraschino Cherries
½ pint of rye whiskey

2 pints of sweet tea
1 pint of brown sugar
1 pint of orange juice
1 pint of lemon juice

Mix, cover and refrigerate for two days. Serve by the glass, mixing in champagne.

On Sunday, May 15, though there was still plenty of sandy terrain ahead, the Washington cavalcade was moving away from the coastal topography and vegetation. Years later, in a letter dated December 11, 1796, Washington revealed his feelings about some of the places he had recently seen and traveled through, "Towards the seaboard of all the Southern states (and further South the more so) the country is low, sandy, and unhealthy, for which reason I shall say little concerning them, for as I should not choose to be an inhabitant of them myself, I ought not say anything that would induce others to be so."

Washington watched and fretted about the horses as they trod up the gradually increasing elevation through sand and loose soil following routes not too far from the Savannah River. Now mid-May, it was probably a warm day, though the president made no remark about the temperature. The travelers knew that the increasing incline through the loose soil was tough on the horses. It was easy to focus on the horses, as there wasn't much else to see in this thinly populated region. On May 16, the travelers stopped for the night at Pearce's Inn in Screven County after an unusually long day of forty-two miles.

The Pearces, Joshua and Hannah and their six children, had settled in Screven in 1768 and shortly thereafter opened their inn. The story at Pearce's goes that Mrs. Pearce prepared a large chicken pie for the president. Three generations of Pearces had operated the inn, and even Lafayette stayed there on his 1825 tour of America.

Uphill but undaunted, the travelers covered forty-three miles on Tuesday, the seventeenth, ending up in Waynesboro, Georgia, namesake of General "Mad Anthony" Wayne, a Pennsylvanian known for his brash, fearless style as a commander during the American Revolution. Waynesboro was established by the Georgia General Assembly in 1783 to honor Wayne. It is not clear if the president even knew it was named for Wayne, but he noted it was the seat of the Burke County court and had only six or eight dwellings.

Waynesboro is much larger today. I was there on a Sunday, and the local eateries were hopping with after-church diners. Washington would be impressed with a prominent American Legion Post in Waynesboro; it displays a head-turning early model jet aircraft out front. The American Legion was founded by veterans of World War I, but Washington likely would be disappointed to learn of the United States' innumerable adventures in "foreign entanglements," something he spoke against in his presidential farewell.

The Woodpecker Trail passes near Waynesboro. Established in 1947 by the Woodpecker Route Association, the route traces its origins to the early days of motoring in the 1920s. The trail is a scenic and historic route through many pine forests—presumably the home of woodpeckers—originally from Charlotte, North Carolina, to St. Petersburg, Florida. The trail is no longer marked in South Carolina or Florida but, apparently, is well-marked in Georgia. I saw a number of the trail's distinctive signs along U.S. 25 between Waynesboro and Augusta. The Trail Association hopes to one day reinstitute the full course of the trail.

Rolling thirty-two miles on Wednesday, May 18, the caravan arrived in Augusta. About four miles outside of town, the entourage was met by Georgia governor Edward Telfair and other dignitaries. Their meeting spot

The president's entourage was met by Georgia governor Edward Telfair at this spot outside Augusta, Georgia. *Author's collection.*

is marked today by a small granite monument and brass plaque hard by Georgia Route 56, the Old Savannah Road.

General Sherman of Civil War fame skipped Augusta, but still, it has suffered ruinous fires, especially one in 1916 that destroyed much of downtown. Augusta's main drag, Broad Street, was laid out with the original city, and true to its name, it has always been one of America's widest streets. Downtown Augusta is now the vibrant home of the arts and restaurants, including Luigi's Ristorante, which has been serving since 1949.

From downtown, I walked to a number of interesting places: the Augusta Riverwalk, the Augusta History Museum, Historic Augusta in Woodrow Wilson's Boyhood Home and the Morris Art Museum.

At the Augusta History Museum, I learned about Jimmie Dyess, a little-known and unique hero who George Washington would admire. Dyess was a big, red-headed, athletic Presbyterian with long family ties to Augusta. His family actually lived across the Savannah River in neighboring North Augusta, South Carolina.

In July 1928, during his college years at Clemson, where he played football, Dyess saved two women from drowning at Sullivan's Island, South Carolina. Dyess did not know the women, and his efforts were incredibly bold and

Naturalist and nurseryman William Bartram of Philadelphia traveled to Savannah and Augusta in the spring of 1773, and coincidentally, he published a book on that trip, *Travels*, in 1791. *Author's collection.*

Future U.S. president Woodrow Wilson was born in Staunton, Virginia, but spent his formative youth in Augusta, Georgia, in this then Presbyterian Church manse. Wilson's father was pastor of First Presbyterian. *Author's collection.*

gallant. He displayed incredible physical strength and presence of mind. Coincidentally, Washington visited Sullivan's Island and its Fort Moultrie during his stay in Charleston.

For his selfless bravery, Dyess received the Andrew Carnegie Medal, awarded to Americans and Canadians who, at the risk of their own life, save or attempt to save the lives of others. The award is granted under exacting standards, and very few earn it.

Dyess finished his studies at Clemson—which in that era was structured much like a military academy—and joined the family lumber business and Augusta civic life. Additionally, throughout the 1930s, Dyess was in the reserve officer corps of first the army and then, later, the Marines. Then came World War II, and Dyess dutifully heeded his country's call, becoming a Marine lieutenant colonel in the Pacific Theater.

On February 2, 1944, Lieutenant Colonel Dyess repeatedly put himself in harm's way while directing his unit's fire, heroically inspiring and leading his Marines in a battle with Japanese in the Marshall Islands. After defying the odds for hours, a burst of enemy machine gun fire killed Dyess instantly. For his remarkable heroism, Dyess was awarded the Congressional Medal of Honor.

Jimmie Dyess is unique: he is the only person ever to receive both the Carnegie Medal and the Congressional Medal of Honor. And in another coincidence, Dyess is honored at the Congressional Medal of Honor Museum at Patriot's Point on the Cooper River, Charleston, South Carolina, roughly where Washington was rowed across those waters when he arrived in the city.

While in Augusta, I had hoped to meet with history professor Dr. Ed Cashin. Sadly, he suddenly died a few months before my visit. Professor Cashin was an expert in Georgia history and had written a number of books, including *The Story of Augusta*. We had exchanged a couple of e-mails about my visit and, in particular, his thoughts about an old story on George Washington's greyhound, Cornwallis. Local legend suggests that while Washington was in Augusta, Cornwallis died and was laid to rest. Some contend that Cornwallis did not die. Others question even the existence of such a hound. Dr. Cashin indicated that the Cornwallis story would forever remain uncertain. I do know that Washington loved dogs, and the Cornwallis story makes a great dog tail, um, tale.

Washington spent three nights in Augusta, and no one is sure of where he stayed. While there, he was celebrated in the customary ways, and of course, he met with Governor Telfair and toured the city and its sites, including the orphanage and Academy of Richmond County, which was established in 1783 and, though now a public school, still operates by that name.

Augusta is at the fall line, and Washington traveled a short distance up the Savannah River to see the falls. The president opined that "the falls are nothing more than rapids and were passable in their present state by boats with skillful hands, but may at a very small expense be improved by removing a few rocks to straighten the passage." Essentially, Washington saw rivers as streams of commerce, and he wanted goods to travel to and fro inland as far as possible.

Chapter 7

GOING NORTH FROM GEORGIA

AUGUSTA TO MOUNT VERNON

On Saturday, May 21, Washington's caravan turned north to cross the bridge over the Savannah River into South Carolina. Washington was thankful for the luxury of the bridge over the Savannah but was probably less thrilled to meet several officials from South Carolina who had arrived as escorts. The lead escort was another officer from the Revolution who was presently a sheriff, Wade Hampton of Columbia, a noted soldier, planter and future congressman. Hampton was the patriarch of a long line of prominent men who would lead South Carolina throughout the next century.

The travelers left Augusta at six o'clock in the morning and traveled forty miles that day. Their route to Columbia was at least partially on the old Two Notch Road. Like a similarly named route in central Virginia, Three Chopt Road, these road names derived from the distinctive number of notches in trees or posts that marked their path. The origin of the expression to "blaze a trail" is quite literal.

Much of the route from Augusta to Columbia kept the travelers west of present-day Interstate 20 and U.S. 1. The area is lightly settled to this day; however, nearby Aiken is a thriving place that benefits from a combination of federal workers at the U.S. Department of Energy's Savannah River site, tourism, retirees and a small state university. Aiken features a charming, perhaps tony, downtown that, until a few years ago, featured a squash shop that didn't sell vegetables but instead catered to enthusiasts of the racquet sport. Polo is also played here. Now that's tony.

On Sunday the twenty-second, there was no mention of departure time, but clearly, the entourage departed early as they traveled all the way to Columbia, covering at least forty-five miles with one of the horses going lame en route. To actually arrive in Columbia, the travelers were relieved with an uneventful ferry trip across the Congaree River as dusk neared. The president then mounted Prescott, and the entourage rode impressively into South Carolina's capital.

Columbia is a planned city, created by the South Carolina General Assembly in 1786, with its location generally central in the state. The legislature first met there in the new statehouse in January 1790. On Monday, Washington had dinner with Columbia's leading citizens at the statehouse, and then a ball followed that night. Washington was not too beleaguered to count the gender of the evening's attendees. The president noted that about 150 gathered for the evening, of which about 50 or 60 were ladies.

On Tuesday, the twenty-fourth, Washington reluctantly opted to spend another day and night in Columbia to allow his foundered horse more time to heal. No doubt with that gimpy horse in his thoughts, Washington wrote, "The whole road from Augusta to Columbia is a pine barren of the worst sort, being hilly as well as poor. This circumstance added to the distance, length of the stages, want of water and heat of the day, foundered one of my horses badly."

Very little, if anything, survives of the tiny Columbia that Washington saw in 1791. Much of Columbia burned in 1865 as Sherman's troops raided the important Confederate city. Included in the ruins was the original statehouse, a wooden structure. The current capitol building is adjacent to the site of the original statehouse, and an image of Washington is prominent on the site.

On the grounds of the South Carolina statehouse stands a bronze replica, created in the mid-nineteenth century, of Antoine Houdon's renowned original marble statue of Washington. With the original likeness in Richmond and replicas in D.C., Raleigh and Columbia, George Washington remains well-remembered throughout the states of his Southern Tour.

In modern Columbia, one of my favorite buildings is a gem from 1940, the Wade Hampton State Office Building. The six-story building mixes elements of classical and Art Deco design; in 2007, the building was listed on the National Register of Historic Places. A friend of mine, who has spent her life in Georgia and the Carolinas, is, on her mother's side, a descendant of the Wade Hampton family. She named one of her daughters Hampton. All three of her daughters' names honor their ancestors. I have no data to support it, but I suspect such honoring by name occurs more in the South.

Columbia was the last state capital visited on the tour. By this point, Washington had paid homage in four state capitals—Annapolis, Richmond, Augusta and Columbia—and had met with the governors of those states. He had been with South Carolina governor Charles Pinckney in Charleston instead of Columbia. North Carolina had no true capital to visit, but he decided to see Governor Martin of that state as he traveled north.

The travelers had left Philadelphia more than sixty days earlier. They were getting tired, and the stops and celebrations were tedious. The key Charleston visit was well behind them, and now they were well out of line with any regular mail in the event that Philadelphia or Mount Vernon wanted to get word to Washington. With no remaining state capitals to visit and no real cities left on the itinerary, the tenor and pace of the trip changed. Much like a baseball umpire's strike zone widens in meaningless late-season games, Washington and the travelers were now less into details and formalities. The president just wanted to keep moving toward Philadelphia—or at least Mount Vernon. They would be courteous and still see and be seen, but they would be on the move, rarely spending more than one night at any stop en route north.

The entourage rolled at its earliest hour yet on Wednesday, May 25—part of the change of tenor. Washington left Columbia at 4:00 a.m. with the foundered horse being led every step of the way. Traveling thirty-six miles, plus a ferry ride across the Wateree River, the group arrived at its next stop, Camden, around 2:00 p.m. Washington was greeted by the town's dignitaries, who read a formal address welcoming the president. With Major Jackson's counsel, Washington's response addressed the significant battles of the Revolution fought in or near Camden as he offered, "May you largely participate the national advantages, and may your past sufferings, and dangers, endured and braved in the cause of freedom, be long contrasted with future safety and happiness."

While in Camden, Washington toured the battlefields of the Revolution and enjoyed a dinner with Camden's finest in a private home that still stands, the Chesnut House. John Chesnut was a veteran of the Revolution, a strong Federalist and a planter specializing in indigo. In addition to enjoying a long festive evening—reports are that Washington stayed until midnight—the president and Chesnut found time to discuss their agricultural interests.

Camden is a great place to visit, with its vibrant downtown along with plenty of historical sites and antique shops. Camden lies on U.S. 1 connecting it with Columbia to the south and the famous golf resorts of North Carolina, Pinehurst and Southern Pines to the north. Each spring, Camden hosts a

Washington was entertained at a private reception in this house, the home of John Chesnut, a Camden, South Carolina indigo planter and veteran of the American Revolution. The home is privately owned and is not open to visitors. *Author's collection.*

popular horse steeplechase, the Carolina Cup. Steeplechases combine speed with jumping ability; I imagine George Washington would have enjoyed watching some of the Carolina Cup.

After the preceding long day, Washington set a gentler pace as his Camden visit extended a bit into the morning of the twenty-sixth. Once underway, Washington stopped at the grave of Johann DeKalb, who was German-born but had ties to the French army and had been a general for the American cause in the Revolution. DeKalb saw extensive duty up and down eastern American—even in Canada—before dying in August 1780 in the Battle of Camden. Around 1825, DeKalb's remains were reinterred in Camden's Bethesda Presbyterian Church on none other than DeKalb Street.

Perhaps Washington noted the symmetry as he tallied that the travelers had logged twenty-six miles on May 26 before lodging at James Ingram's in Lancaster County, a little south of present-day Heath Springs, South Carolina. I find no mention of the once lame horse, but I am left to guess that he was stepping much better by this day.

On Friday and Saturday, the twenty-seventh and twenty-eight, departure time was 4:00 a.m. Following roughly present-day U.S. 521, the northbound

Above: Robert Mills, a Charleston native and one of America's first native-born professional architects, designed the Kershaw County Courthouse in Camden, South Carolina, in 1825. Mills also designed the Washington monuments of Baltimore and Washington, D.C. *Author's collection.*

Right: Shortly after departing Camden, South Carolina, Washington stopped to pay his respects to a fallen hero of the American Revolution. *Author's collection.*

Washington paid for his meal at Nathan Barr's Tavern in Lancaster County, South Carolina, with a Spanish coin that he chiseled in two. The half-coin was long cherished by the Barr family before it was bequeathed to Wofford College in the late 1800s. *Courtesy of Wofford College.*

caravan was on a roll with little ceremony as they neared the Old North State—North Carolina.

On Friday, the president reluctantly met with Catawba Indian leaders, who were concerned that white settlers would ultimately encroach and make claims on the 144,000 acres of land reserved for them by the Continental Congress in the 1763 Treaty of Augusta. The Indian lands covered much of present-day towns Rock Hill and Fort Mill, South Carolina. Washington listened to the Catawba chiefs but took no stand, apparently considering enforcement of their treaty a matter for South Carolina.

May 27, 1791, was Washington's last night in South Carolina; the travelers arrived in Charlotte at about three o'clock in the afternoon on May 28. If Washington had any particular thoughts about his time in South Carolina, he did not record them in his diary. He was, however, pleased to finally get out of the "piney sandy soils" shortly after leaving Camden. Sandy soil and dust-stirring, curious militia escorts were two of Washington's greatest annoyances on the tour.

"Charlotte is a very trifling place," opined President Washington in his diary entry for Saturday, May 28. Charlotte was the courthouse town for

Right: Charlotte is a thriving city, but it was an unimpressive county seat when Washington visited in 1791. The Elmwood Cemetery includes the remains of native son and movie actor Randolph Scott, while uptown is headquarters of Bank of America. *Author's collection.*

Below: Washington didn't visit the Hezekiah Alexander home in Charlotte, though it was built around 1774 and was continuously used as a residence until around 1950. Today, the "Rock House" is part of the Charlotte Museum of History. *Author's collection.*

Mecklenburg County, and at that time, the courthouse literally stood in the main intersection of the town, Trade and Tryon Streets. Today, the intersection remains, but instead of ramshackle buildings and dust, it is surrounded by glistening skyscrapers, an NBA arena and an NFL stadium. Charlotte has great civic pride and is anything but trifling.

Washington's host in Charlotte was Thomas Polk, a great-uncle to future U.S. president James K. Polk. Though Polk attended the president about Charlotte, the legend goes that Washington actually lodged at Cook's Inn at the corner of Church and Trade Streets, where he left his powder box behind. No, not gunpowder—powder for his hair. Powder was part of a gentleman's grooming in that era. In a time when bathing was inconvenient, if not impossible, powdering the hair gave it a fresher, cleaner appearance.

I don't know what happened to the powder box, but I do know that Washington left it behind on one of his relatively leisurely mornings, as the entourage did not depart Charlotte until 7:00 a.m. Perhaps Washington slowed it down for the Sabbath; it was, after all, Sunday, May 29. The group passed near present-day Charlotte Motor Speedway en route to spend a night at Red Hill, the farmstead of Martin Phifer, a little west of present-day Concord. A historical marker near the intersection of U.S. 29 and Poplar Tent Road reminds passersby that Washington slept nearby.

Monday, May 30, brought a new week and a return to the 4:00 a.m. departure time as the caravan saddled up for a short twenty-mile trip to Salisbury. Washington liked these lands, which were red soil this deep into the Piedmont. The entourage came along present-day U.S. 29/601 as it neared

Legend has it that President Washington stopped at the Richard Brandon home before proceeding to welcoming festivities in Salisbury, North Carolina. *Author's collection.*

town. Lore suggests that the group stopped for a break a few miles from town at the home of a Mr. Brandon, but regardless, it arrived in Salisbury in time for breakfast. Soon, a day of festivities ensued featuring a parade, a tea, a dinner and likely a ball.

Salisbury developed along a key trading path and was always a busy place in backcountry North Carolina. Today it is situated on Interstate 85, and U.S.

The Washington Building was built in the early twentieth century on the site of the former Yarborough Hotel, which Washington at least visited during his time in Salisbury, North Carolina. *Author's collection.*

The Archibald Henderson Law Office in Salisbury, North Carolina, was built in 1796. In the 1920s, the lawyer's Salisbury descendant of the same name wrote a book on Washington's 1791 Southern Tour. *Author's collection.*

These steps are kept on the grounds of the Rowan Public Library in Salisbury, North Carolina, and it has long been said that Washington stood on them during his visit. Others say that the steps date to the early nineteenth century. *Author's collection.*

Routes 29, 70, 601 and 52 all pass through it. U.S. 52 is the one highway that North Carolina and North Dakota have in common; the route goes from Charleston, South Carolina, to Bowbells, North Dakota. Many of these routes are used by delivery trucks of the popular soft drink company Cheerwine, which has produced a special-formula, cherry-flavored cola in Salisbury since 1917.

While in Salisbury, Washington saw framed paintings of King George III and his consort, Queen Charlotte. These particular portraits would hold a special fascination for Washington. The town was whipsawed in the Revolution by passing forces from both sides, but most locals stayed true to the American cause. The portraits hung at Steel's Tavern in Salisbury; the Steels were ancestors of Archibald Henderson, the 1920s author of *Washington's Southern Tour*.

On a visit to Steels' in 1781, American general Nathanael Greene, upon receiving great encouragement from the innkeeper, Mrs. Elizabeth Maxwell Steele, wrote on the back of King George's portrait: "O George—Hide thy face and mourn." Washington was surely amused at this discovery, and it had to rekindle his warm feelings for General Greene. The portraits are now at the Thyatira Presbyterian Church on North Carolina Route 150, a few miles southwest of town. The 260-year old congregation maintains a small museum that opens upon appointment.

At 4:00 a.m. on May 31, Washington launched from Salisbury and headed north to Long's Ferry to cross the Yadkin River. Modern bridges now span the Yadkin, but not far from Interstate 85, there's still a Long's Ferry Road, and ferryman Alexander Long's fine home from 1786 still stands. The private home features distinctive markings in the chimneys; glazed bricks were used to form hearts and the couples' initials to signify their marriage.

Washington's path toward Salem, a Moravian community now known as Old Salem, roughly followed present-day North Carolina Route 150. A friend, whose family has long held land near where Washington passed along that road, has established a vineyard on it and plans to market the wine under the name "Southern Tour." I'll drink to that—just not fifteen toasts.

The entourage, which a month ago had spent a day riding just above sea level at present-day Myrtle Beach and then through South Carolina's Lowcountry, now found themselves in the tour's peak elevation. For the next few days, they traveled a portion of Piedmont North Carolina at elevations ranging from seven hundred to one thousand feet.

Somewhere along the way, three Moravian ministers intersected Washington and led the entourage to Salem. As they arrived in the little

Left: President Washington may have taken a seat on this stone when the travelers rested in Reeds, North Carolina. In 1926, the Daughters of the American Revolution from nearby Lexington turned the large stone upright and made it a monument. *Author's collection.*

Below: Salem Tavern in present-day Old Salem, North Carolina, was built in 1784. Washington spent two nights here and especially enjoyed traditional Moravian music. *Author's collection.*

community with a population of around 220, they were serenaded with music. Moravians are known for their music, especially their use of various horns. Washington was likely delighted with the respectful but relatively low-key reception—no militia—that featured families gathered in the village center. Washington remained in his chariot until the caravan stopped in the village. He then alighted and reportedly took great pleasure in mingling with those gathered, including the children.

The president was less pleased to receive news that North Carolina governor Alexander Martin had sent word that he wished to greet the president at Salem but that he could not arrive until the afternoon of June 1—twenty-four hours later. Washington had nothing against Salem, but the president's string of one-night stands would now be broken, and that he lamented.

Top: The tour guides dress in period attire at Old Salem, North Carolina. *Author's collection.*

Right: In 1932, Old Salem, North Carolina, commemorated President Washington's visit with a pageant. Over fifteen thousand attended with over five hundred in costume. Even North Carolina governor O. Max Gardner (right) participated. *Courtesy of Moravian Archives.*

Nonetheless, Washington much enjoyed additional meals, music and tours in Salem and was especially taken by the well-engineered water works that distributed water in the village. The Moravians discovered and tapped a nearby spring that today lends its name to Winston-Salem's Spring Street.

On Thursday, June 2, Governor Martin likely began his day earlier than usual as he was traveling with President Washington, who took no prisoners at departure time. Once again, it was 4:00 a.m. Everyone moved when Washington said move. The group stopped for breakfast at Dobson's Tavern near present-day Kernersville before completing the day at Guilford Courthouse, which is now at the northwestern edge of Greensboro. Though it was Martha Washington's sixtieth birthday, the president made no record in his diary of his beloved's special occasion.

Governor Martin had a home in the small village of Guilford Courthouse or, as it was then known, Martinville—apparently named for the governor. Guilford Courthouse was the site of a significant battle in 1781, a battle that some say was the beginning of the end for the British in the Revolution.

Technically, the British won the battle at Guilford, but they suffered great casualties in the process, both physical and emotional. Depleted physically and

President Washington enjoyed refreshment from this pewterware during a stop at Ballinger's Tavern in Guilford County, North Carolina. *Courtesy of Greensboro Historical Museum.*

This monument to the cavalry was erected at the Guilford Courthouse, North Carolina battleground in 1910. Among those honored is President Washington's cousin, Colonel William Washington. *Author's collection.*

spiritually and a long way from their supplies, the British never recovered. The following fall, General Cornwallis surrendered to Washington at Yorktown, Virginia, when trapped by the Continental army and French navy. Washington was pleased to look over this important battle site.

Governor Martin assured Washington that North Carolina was coming along nicely as a new state and that its people's acceptance of the federal government and even the new tax on whiskey production was generally favorable. Washington spent the night with Martin, but the governor and all the travelers were up early once again, as the caravan rolled at four o'clock in the morning. Governor Martin requested to attend the president all the way to the Virginia line, but Washington relieved him of any sense of such duty.

On Friday, June 3, Washington had seen his last governor of the trip and was nearing Virginia. Generally, the formal part of the Southern Tour was over. From here to Mount Vernon and from Mount Vernon to Philadelphia, there would be only relatively subdued ceremony and celebration. As it relates to the essence of the tour, Washington now had the sense of a mission accomplished.

The travelers had probably endured some warm weather in recent weeks, which would only worsen as the June days passed. On June 3, as they traveled through Rockingham and Caswell Counties, their path came under some rain, which had been so rare in this year of drought. After about forty-five miles, Washington stopped about two miles shy of the Virginia state line and spent the night with Mr. Dudley Gatewood, very close to present-day North Carolina Route 86. It was George Washington's last night in North Carolina.

On the morning of June 4, Washington eased across the Virginia state line around seven o'clock and, shortly thereafter, was ferrying across the Dan River. At some point that day, he posted in his diary a long entry of his reflections and observations on the Carolinas and Georgia. Some of Washington's words:

> *Having this day passed the line of No. Carolina, and of course finished my tour thro' the three Southernmost States a general description of them may be comprised in the few following words.*
>
> *From the Sea board to the falls of all the Rivers which water this extensive region, the lands, except the Swamps, on the rivers, and the lesser streams which empty into them; & the interval lands higher up the Rivers is, with but few exceptions, neither more nor less than a continued pine barren very thinly inhabited. The part next the Sea board, for many miles, is a dead level & badly watered. That above it is hilly & not much better watered, but if possible, less valuable on account of its hilliness and because they are more inconvenient to markets.*
>
> *The lands above the falls of the several Rivers from information, and as far as my own observations has extended, is of a very superior kinds from these being of a greasy red, with large oaks, intermixed with hickory chestnut & ca. producing, corn, Tobo., Wheat, Hemp & other articles in great abundances & are generally thickly inhabited comparatively speaking with those below.*
>
> *Excepting the Towns (and some Gentlemans Seats along the Road from Charleston to Savannah) there is not, within view of the whole road I*

travelled from Petersburgh to this place, a single house which has anything of an elegant appearance. They are altogether of Wood & chiefly of logs—some have brick chimneys but generally the chimnies are of Split sticks filled with dirt between them.

The accommodations on the whole Road (except in the Towns, and even there, as I was informed for I had no opportunity of Judging, lodgings having been provided for me in them at my own expense) we found extremely indifferent—the houses being small and badly provided either for man or horse; though extra exertions when it was known I was coming, wch. was generally the case, were made to receive me.

The manners of the people, as far as my observations, and means of information extended, were orderly and Civil. And they appeared to be happy, contented and satisfied with the genl. governmt. under which they were placed. Where the case was otherwise, it was not difficult to trace the cause to some demagogue, or speculating character.

The discontents which it was supposed the last Revenue Act (commonly known as the Excise Law) would create subside as fast as the new law is explained.

For the next eight days, the caravan worked its way northeast through Virginia, passing Halifax Old Town, a now defunct burg in Pittsylvania County, and through parts of Halifax, Charlotte, Prince Edward, Cumberland, Louisa, Goochland, Spotsylvania, Stafford and Prince William Counties before arriving at Mount Vernon in Fairfax County on Sunday, June 12.

During this Virginia stretch north, Washington did take advantage of some private hospitality. He took two days for a little extra rest in Halifax County at the home of former congressman Isaac Coles. Everyone benefitted, including the horses, as they took advantage of Coles's fine pasture. A descendant of Isaac Coles has been in the news in recent years as one of the leaders seeking to overturn Virginia's ban on uranium mining. It turns out that this region is rich in uranium, the metallic chemical element that helps fuel nuclear energy plants. The uranium is beneath the soil, but on the surface, Washington would still see lovely land and green pastures in this part of Virginia.

The staff may have enjoyed easier days while the horses grazed at Coles's estate, but they didn't get to lodge there; instead, they were put up at nearby taverns, all of which had poor reputations. Among the area taverns was Priddy's; Washington stopped there for breakfast on June 5.

The bed where Washington slept during his stay with Isaac Coles in Southside Virginia is still in the Coles family. *Author's collection.*

The traveling congressman William Loughton Smith, en route south, had just stayed at Priddy's Tavern a month earlier. Smith's journal for May 3, 1791, reads:

> *I put up this night at one Pridie's, a sorry tavern; I had for company an idiot, the landlord's brother, who was himself but one remove from it…My fare was indifferent, and as I was kept awake a great part of the night by bugs and fleas, and the united groaning and grunting of the hogs under the window, and my man Ben in the chamber with me, all this agreeable music was enlivened by perpetual peals of thunder and the rattling of heavy rain on the shingles over my head, which continued nearly the whole night, and began just as I entered the tavern.*

Perhaps this part of Virginia had been a bit more blessed with rain, making Isaac Coles's pastures so attractive for Washington's horses.

Washington's visit to Charlotte Courthouse caused quite a stir in the rural area, with almost everyone being alert for a chance to see the president or

Above: Tobacco barns and various other examples of vernacular architecture dot Southside Virginia, the central Virginia region to the south of the James River. *Author's collection.*

Right: Historical markers line U.S. Route 15 in Worsham, Virginia. One marker notes that President Washington was a guest in the community in June 1791. *Author's collection.*

Above: Washington was involved in myriad ways at Pohick Church, but he didn't stop on Sunday, June 12, 1791, as he made his way north to Mount Vernon. *Author's collection.*

Left: This baptismal font has been part of Pohick Church since the 1700s. The font dates to eleventh- or twelfth-century England. *Author's collection.*

the passing entourage. The president had breakfast in Charlotte Courthouse, where a farrier also replaced some missing horseshoes on a few of the horses.

The travelers eventually pushed forward past the edge of Hampden-Sydney College before spending a night in Prince Edward Courthouse, now known as Worsham. The county seat moved to Farmville in 1872. Worsham is a small collection of buildings smack-dab on U.S. 15; a few years ago while poking around Worsham, I spoke to some folks at a country store and to a sheriff's deputy. None realized that George Washington had slept there. They thought I was kidding, but a historical marker just down the road confirmed my point.

On Sunday, June 12, Washington rode right past one of his churches as he neared Mount Vernon. However, the president made no mention of Pohick Church, which is still an active Episcopal congregation in a red-brick, circa 1770 building hard by U.S. 1. The president was probably just thinking about getting home; his diary noted that he would be "at home" until Monday, June 27, the day of an appointment with the federal district commissioners in George Town. The travelers would hold up at Mount Vernon for two weeks.

Chapter 8

MOUNT VERNON TO PHILADELPHIA

O ver the two weeks at Mount Vernon, Washington and William Jackson refocused on the affairs of government and received and produced considerable official correspondence. Additionally, Washington kept happy and busy in riding the farms and evaluating their productivity and the condition of the estate in general. Washington always had a keen eye for detail; I suspect he ordered some fence mending and whitewashing.

The servants from the tour were likely put to work around the house since the Washingtons now lived in Philadelphia; things were not up and running as usual in the Mount Vernon household. In essence, these men continued to serve the president much as they had throughout the tour as valet and footmen. Coachman Fagan probably took on various tasks and made sure the caravan's horses remained in good shape. Washington let no resource go to waste, so I know he kept them busy.

The president had increasingly become annoyed with Paris during the tour, apparently displeased with his attitude. Paris was only in his early twenties, and Giles was thirty-something. The president decided to leave both at Mount Vernon, and neither ever returned to Philadelphia. Paris died from an illness in 1794, and Giles, too, died at some point during the 1790s; both were probably interred in Mount Vernon's slave burial ground just a short distance from George and Martha Washington's tomb.

Before 6:00 a.m. on Monday, June 27, the travelers were underway, bound for a 9:00 a.m. meeting with the federal district commissioners. The meeting probably happened at Suter's Tavern in Georgetown. To get to Suter's,

Left: Washington commissioned a "Dove of Peace" weathervane to sit atop Mount Vernon. *Author's collection.*

Below: The Old Stone House in the Georgetown section of Washington, D.C., dates to the 1760s. Washington passed the home frequently during his visits to the federal city. It is now a National Park Service site. *Author's collection.*

Washington would pass over Rock Creek on present-day M Street and pass a simple circa 1765 home on his right that today is known as the Old Stone House, a National Park Service site. The Old Stone House is thought to be the oldest unaltered house in D.C. It is open for touring most days. This property may be the only remaining building in D.C. that Washington passed on his visits during the Southern Tour.

After a review of plans with the commissioners, Washington met with landowners in follow-up to their meeting back in late March. Despite contentiousness from some owners who were either concerned about the size of the proposed federal district or how they were affected by the financial arrangements, an irked Washington pushed and promoted the need for landowner cooperation, appealing to their common sense and patriotism. Washington made his point, and arrangements were made for the necessary owners to sign deeds effectuating the deal over the following two days. The federal government would soon have the necessary parcel needed for its new capital.

Washington spent the next two days riding the district, spending time with L'Enfant and Ellicott, the designer and surveyor. They considered the lay of the land and site lines; Washington, the old surveyor, was right at home. But Washington was also the chief executive of "operation Federal City," and in consultation with these men and, apparently at the suggestion of L'Enfant, by June 29, the locations of the executive department and of the legislative building had been determined. Today, we know them as the White House and Capitol Building.

On Thursday, June 30, at 4:00 a.m., Washington, the happy and triumphant capital city deal-maker, left George Town. Desiring to see Frederick, Maryland, and the Pennsylvania burgs of York and Lancaster, Washington "prosecuted" his return to Philadelphia through those places—avoiding any more nasty encounters on the Chesapeake Bay.

The travelers stopped for breakfast in Williamsburg, Maryland—now known as Rockville—and arrived in Frederick around 7:30 p.m. It was still daylight on this long summer day, and the citizens of Frederick rallied with church bells and cannon salutes. Washington couldn't get out of town the following morning without hearing an address from the approving citizens of Frederick, but he still managed to leave around seven o'clock.

I don't know Washington's route to his next stop, but it likely tracked close to present-day Maryland Route 194 up to Taneytown. It's a pretty drive today, and Washington liked what he saw, noting that the land was "remarkably fine." Washington was not to be detained in Taneytown; he

Black Horse Tavern in York, Pennsylvania, was operated for decades by the Spangler family. The tavern hosted Washington on July 2–3, 1791. In 1777, the Articles of Confederation were drafted here by the Continental Congress. *Author's collection.*

was off by four o'clock on the morning of July 2, crossing the line into Pennsylvania in about six miles.

Washington wound up in York, Pennsylvania, at the end of the day, a day that led him right into Sunday and another chance to attend a church service before closing the circle of the Southern Tour. Perhaps a bit sarcastically, Washington wrote, "There being no Episcopal minister present in this place, I went to hear morning service performed in the Dutch Reformed Church—which, being in that language not a word of which I understood I was in no danger of becoming a proselyte to its religion by the eloquence of the preacher." The service was at the German Reformed Church, which burned down before the next century. Washington spelled "Deutsch" as "Dutch," demonstrating how Pennsylvania Deutsch became commonly known as Pennsylvania Dutch.

That afternoon, escorted by a small delegation from York, the travelers made tracks toward Lancaster, crossing the Susquehanna River on Wright's Ferry. By now, less than one hundred miles away, the president had to be happily thinking about getting back to life in Philadelphia and seeing Martha. Perhaps he even overlooked the dust stirred by the York escort. Washington, who knew a good river view when he saw one,

Prospect Hill Cemetery in York, Pennsylvania, a site with over ninety thousand graves, is decorated with American flags for a Veterans Day tribute. *Author's collection.*

noted that the Susquehanna was more than one mile wide where they crossed with "pretty views on the banks of it." Travelers today crossing the river heading east on U.S. Route 30 see a similar beauty to what Washington beheld. The president, unlike on other occasions, made no complaint about the ferry ride; it must have been smooth sailing. I think Washington had a good day.

Monday, July 4, 1791, was the fifteenth anniversary of American independence, and President Washington was in Lancaster, Pennsylvania. Lancaster's citizens probably felt divinely blessed by their good fortune to have—by chance—George Washington in town for the Fourth of July. As we might say today, "Are you kidding me?" The president agreed to spend the day in town for the festivities and celebration.

Washington's diary for the Southern Tour ends on July 4. He does not record if he stayed a second night in Lancaster or continued east late that day. By his diary account, we know he was still in Lancaster well into late afternoon. I speculate that he stayed another night in Lancaster, leaving, say, at four or five o'clock the following morning.

However, he did not arrive in Philadelphia until sometime into the day of July 6. To date, I've not been able to determine where George Washington slept on either July 4 or July 5, 1791. That's just the sort of mystery I enjoy investigating.

Chapter 9

REFLECTIONS ON THE SOUTHERN TOUR

W ashington arrived in Philadelphia on July 6 to waving crowds, ringing bells and artillery salutes. When the chariot arrived back at the president's home, the legend goes that one of the Clark brothers, the carriage-maker, was on hand proudly inspecting his well-traveled vehicle. Coachman Fagan assured him it had served well and that every bolt was tight.

The chariot indeed held up well, and after having a couple of weeks to consider it, Washington had surely concluded that the trip was worth all the trouble and wear and tear on equipment, man and beast.

On July 20, he wrote his friend David Humphreys, who served as an aide-de-camp to Washington in the Revolution. Among other topics, Washington waxed a good deal about his recent Southern Tour of 1887 miles and about the general state of the American government:

> *I am much pleased that I have taken this journey as it has enabled me to see with my own eyes the situation of the country thro' which we travelled, and to learn more accurately the disposition of the people than I could have done by any information.*
>
> *The country appears to be in an improving state, and industry and frugality are becoming much more fashionable than that have hitherto been there—Tranquility reigns among the people, with that disposition towards the general government which is likely to preserve it—They begin to feel the good effects of equal laws and equal protection—The farmer finds a ready market for his produce, and the merchant calculates more certainty on*

This present-day corner of Market and Sixth Street in Philadelphia is in the city's historic center. The Southern Tour began and ended here, then the site of the president's home. In 1791, Market Street was High Street. *Author's collection.*

> *his payments—Manufacturers have as yet made little progress in that part of the country…*
>
> *Each days experience of the Government of the United States seems to confirm its establishment, and to render it more popular—A ready acquiescence in the laws made under it shews in a strong light the confidence the people have in their representatives, and in the upright views in those who administer the government.*

Of course, of those administering the federal government, few citizens believed and trusted anyone more than George Washington. His appearance in the thirteen states in timely fashion after his assumption of the presidency did much to build trust, assuage fears and unite the country. The tours were an emotional boost for a fledgling nation.

Of the tours, the Southern Tour was as remarkable a physical feat as it was a political one. Today, many who are aware of the Southern Tour think of it mainly in terms of Washington's visit to their town or state, not realizing the extent of the president's long, sustained journey.

The great planner Washington assembled a good staff, good horses and good equipment. The travelers were fortunate that there were no injuries during the incidents on the Chesapeake and Occoquan Creek. Except for taking an extra day in Columbia to rest a hobbled horse, the group lost no time to illness or injury.

We may never know if Cornwallis the greyhound was part of the journey or if Washington really left his hair powder in Charlotte, but such stories sustain the legacy of the Southern Tour. Folktales and ancillary adventures like the Southern Tour enliven the otherwise serious study of matters like the Constitution and taxation.

In addition to commemorations already mentioned, there have been others over the years that have helped sustain interest in the Southern Tour. New Bern re-created Washington's Ball in April 1891, and in the spring of 2015, New Bern's civic and heritage leaders staged an entire weekend of activities dubbed "President Washington's Second Southern Tour." And at some point, scores of years ago, Camden re-created its evening with the president; the local library has some information on that event.

One of the largest gingko trees in the United States is on the grounds of the circa 1801 Old Government House in Augusta; the tree was supposedly planted with the new building to commemorate Washington's visit. In 1925, North Carolina's Daughters of the American Revolution (DAR) planted trees, each with a commemorative marker, in nine of the Tar Heel communities visited by Washington. Mrs. William Neal Reynolds, of Winston-Salem's notable tobacco family, donated the trees.

The Heyward-Washington House in Charleston, where Washington lodged, was one of the first acquired by that city's preservationists back in 1929. It is well maintained and open to the public. In recent years, the South Carolina Society of the Cincinnati reenacted its Charleston dinner with Washington in a restored McCrady's Tavern, the site of the original festivity. And in 2011, Old Salem had Mount Vernon's official George Washington reenactor come down for a May weekend to celebrate the 220th anniversary of Washington's visit to its Moravian village.

Richard Walser's high school essay on the tour won the 1923 North Carolina DAR annual statewide competition. Walser, who later became a popular member of the English faculty at North Carolina State University, was from Lexington, North Carolina. President Washington passed just a few miles west of Walser's hometown.

Archibald Henderson's large article on the tour, "George Washington Swings the Circle," was published in the *New York Times* on February 19, 1922. Nearly fifty years later in 1971, Roy Parker of the *Winston-Salem Journal* wrote a series of articles on Washington's stops in North Carolina.

The Heyward-Washington House at 87 Church Street was the president's home during his week in Charleston, South Carolina. The home is one of the few extant sites where Washington lodged during the Southern Tour. *Author's collection.*

The tour has generally not gotten much ink in the plethora of Washington biographies, but Ron Chernow's recent excellent volume includes a chapter on the Southern Tour.

In the present day, along the entire route of the tour, some places of Lowcountry South Carolina and of Southside Virginia probably most resemble their appearance of 1791. In Colleton County, South Carolina, the scenery around Fish Pond Bridge on Ritter Road (South Carolina Road 1541) looks remarkably as it did when Washington passed—wild, natural and undeveloped. A beautiful painting from 1790 by artist Thomas Coram, *View from Fish Pond Bridge*, is displayed in Gibbes Museum of Art in Charleston. The painting provides evidence of just how little things have changed at that spot over the last 225 years.

Washington would still recognize aspects of south-central Virginia, a mostly rural land known as Southside, where the black snakes still grow long. Out in the country, where traffic is light and people have an appreciation of how the harmless black rat snake is great for rodent control, these snakes live long lives, often growing to four, five, six or sometimes seven feet long. In urban areas, where all snakes are persecuted, black snakes are lucky to make it to two feet.

The former Hamilton High School near Cartersville, Virginia, was built in 1910. Washington lodged somewhere near here in June 1791 at Moore's Tavern. *Author's collection.*

Blanton & Pleasants has been a family-operated general store in Cartersville, Virginia, since 1929. On several visits to the store, I've not met anyone who was aware that President Washington passed through Cartersville. *Author's collection.*

Some years ago, while touring with a University of Virginia architectural history seminar, an amateur naturalist among us stole away during one of our stops in Southside's pastoral Buckingham County. Our colleague reappeared a few minutes later, trying his best to manage a six-foot black rat snake. While the rest of us were gathered outside in a circle, absorbed by our lead professor's insight on the wonders of that particular estate's front door, the naturalist spied the long serpent and had gone and made the catch. Proving we were mostly a bunch of city slickers, our group broke up amid shrieks and screams when the impressive snake and its handler suddenly appeared.

For lodging, Washington accepted a good deal of private hospitality during the tour. Many were insistent with their invitations to host the president, and due to the lack of convenient or tolerable hostelries, Washington accepted quite a few. He rarely paid for his lodgings along the South Carolina coast. Additionally, the larger communities made arrangements to house Washington at their expense, and some of the small innkeepers refused to accept payment from such a great man.

Of the fifty-eight distinct places he slept, Washington probably paid out of pocket for fewer than half of them. Naturally, he didn't pay for staying in his own bed at Mount Vernon, and he didn't pay for that wet, cramped night

The Southern Tour entourage crossed the James River by ferry somewhere near here in June 1791. The remains of a bridge are that of an 1884 bridge destroyed by Hurricane Agnes in 1972. *Author's collection.*

on the grounded ferry off Annapolis. Regardless of who picked up the tab, overnight stops on the Southern Tour added to the legendary list of places where George Washington slept.

Only seven of the buildings survive in which Washington lodged during the tour—and that includes Mount Vernon. A vestige of an eighth building, the Dudley Gatewood home, Washington's last stop in North Carolina, now stands in Hillsborough, North Carolina; it was deconstructed and moved in the 1970s from its original location just inside the North Carolina–Virginia border. It's uncertain as to how much the rebuilt home is altered from the original.

There are, of course, a few extant buildings that Washington merely visited (and didn't sleep in!). Charleston has the best collection, and ironically, you can sleep in one of them even if Washington didn't—the John Rutledge House on Broad Street is now the John Rutledge House Inn. A short walk from the Rutledge House stand two former Washington haunts, the Exchange Building on East Bay Street and St. Michael's Episcopal Church.

George Washington died in late 1799, and Martha followed in May 1802. George Washington Parke Custis, the president's step-grandson, purchased the Southern Tour chariot from the estate for $610 in 1801. About fifteen years later, the chariot, the veteran artifact of the Southern Tour and other

Washington was entertained in the Charleston home of John Rutledge, a South Carolina governor and judge and a U.S. Supreme Court justice. *Author's collection.*

roads, was by then ramshackle and was acquired by Episcopal Bishop William Meade of Virginia. The chariot was deconstructed and turned into mementoes, such as walking sticks, picture frames and snuff boxes that were sold for charitable purposes.

As mentioned earlier, the two slaves associated with the Southern Tour, Paris and Giles, died in the 1790s and are likely buried at Mount Vernon. I don't know what came of any of the servants—coachman John Fagan; attendants James Hurley, John Mauld and Fiedes Imhoff; and valet William Osborne. Other than with Paris's performance, Washington apparently was pleased with the staff of the Southern Tour.

Major William Jackson, the young man from South Carolina and veteran of the Revolution who had served Washington well at the Constitutional Convention and in two presidential tours, resigned from his secretarial duties later in 1791 to pursue his career in law. Jackson lived mostly in Philadelphia for the rest of his life and married in 1795; Washington attended the wedding. Jackson died at age sixty-nine in 1828. His resting place is Christ Church Burial Ground in Center City Philadelphia—within sight of where the Southern Tour launched back in 1791.

WHERE WASHINGTON SLEPT ON THE SOUTHERN TOUR, 1791

Departed from 190 High Street (the presidential mansion, the present-day corner of Sixth and Market Streets) in Philadelphia, Pennsylvania, at 11:00 a.m. on March 21, 1791.

March 21	Wythe's Inn	Chester, Pennsylvania
March 22	Red Lion Tavern	Red Lion, Delaware
March 23	Worrell's Inn	Chester, Maryland
March 24	aground on the Severn River	offshore from Annapolis, Maryland
March 25–26	Mann's Tavern	Annapolis, Maryland
March 27	Indian Queen Tavern**	Bladensburg, Maryland
March 28–29	Suter's Tavern	George Town, Maryland
March 30–April 6	Mount Vernon*	Fairfax County, Virginia
April 7	unknown	Dumfries, Virginia
April 8–9	Kenmore*	Fredericksburg, Virginia

April 10	Kenner's Tavern	Caroline County, Virginia
April 11–13	Home of Edward Carrington	Richmond, Virginia
April 14	unknown	Petersburg, Virginia
April 15	Oliver's	Sussex County, Virginia
April 16–17	unknown	Halifax, North Carolina
April 18	unknown	Tarboro, North Carolina
April 19	home of Shadrach Allen	Pitt County, North Carolina
April 20–21	home of John Wright Stanly*	New Bern, North Carolina
April 22	Shine's Tavern	Jones County, North Carolina
April 23	Sage's Ordinary	Onslow County, North Carolina
April 24–25	home of John Quince	Wilmington, North Carolina
April 26	Russ's Tavern	Brunswick County, North Carolina
April 27	home of Jeremiah Vereen	Horry County, South Carolina
April 28	Brookgreen Plantation	Horry County, South Carolina
April 29	Clifton Plantation	near Georgetown, South Carolina
April 30	Stewart-Parker House*	Georgetown, South Carolina
May 1	Salt Pond Plantation	near Awendaw, South Carolina
May 2–8	Heyward-Washington House*	Charleston, South Carolina
May 9	Sandy Hill Plantation	Charleston County, South Carolina
May 10	Duharra Plantation	Colleton County, South Carolina
May 11	White Hall Plantation	Beaufort County, South Carolina
May 12–14	unknown property in Telfair Square	Savannah, Georgia
May 15	Spencer's Inn	Effingham County, Georgia
May 16	Pierce's Inn	Screven County, Georgia
May 17	unknown	Waynesboro, Georgia
May 18–20	unknown	Augusta, Georgia
May 21	home of Jacob Odom	near Ridge Spring, South Carolina

May 22–24	unknown	Columbia, South Carolina
May 25	home of Adam F. Brisbane	Camden, South Carolina
May 26	Ingram's Tavern	near Heath Springs, South Carolina
May 27	home of Thomas Crawford	near Van Wyck, South Carolina
May 28	Cook's Inn	Charlotte, North Carolina
May 29	home of Martin Phifer	near present-day Concord, North Carolina
May 30	Hughes's Inn	Salisbury, North Carolina
May 31–June 1	Salem Tavern*	Old Salem, North Carolina
June 2	home of Governor Alexander Martin	Guilford Courthouse, North Carolina
June 3	home of Dudley Gatewood***	Caswell County, North Carolina
June 4	unknown	Pittsylvania County, Virginia
June 5–6	home of Isaac Coles	Halifax County, Virginia
June 7	unknown	Worsham, Virginia
June 8	Moore's Tavern	Cartersville, Virginia
June 9	Jerdone Castle* (private)	Bumpass, Virginia
June 10	Kenmore*	Fredericksburg, Virginia
June 11	unknown	Stafford Court House, Virginia
June 12–June 26	Mount Vernon*	Fairfax County, Virginia
June 27–29	Suter's Tavern	Georgetown, Maryland
June 30	Brother's Tavern	Frederick, Maryland
July 1	unknown	Taneytown, Maryland
July 2	Baltzer Spangler's Tavern	York, Pennsylvania
July 3–4	unknown	Lancaster, Pennsylvania
July 5	unknown	between Lancaster and Philadelphia, Pennsylvania
July 6	arrived in Philadelphia	190 High Street, Philadelphia, Pennsylvania

*Building is extant. All of the extant homes, with the exception of Jerdone Castle, which has always been a private residence, are generally open to the public. However, none of them allows overnight guests.

**The restored building advertised today as Indian Queen Tavern in Bladensburg dates back to the mid-1700s. However, it is thought that the actual tavern building where Washington lodged on several occasions, including the Southern Tour, was a wooden building adjacent to today's remaining property and was torn down long ago. Despite these facts, the remaining structure is referred to as Indian Queen Tavern or, sometimes, the George Washington House.

***Vestiges of the Dudley Gatewood home remain. The property was deconstructed and moved to Hillsborough, North Carolina, in the 1970s and was rebuilt in Daniel Boone Village on Old North Carolina Route 86, just off Interstate 85.

SUGGESTED READINGS

BOOKS

Anderson, Elizabeth B. *Annapolis—A Walk Through History*. 2ⁿᵈ ed. Centreville, MD: Tidewater Publishers, 2003.

Annan, Jason, and Pamela Gabriel. *The Great Cooper River Bridge*. Columbia: University of South Carolina Press, 2002.

Bartram, William. *Travels*. New York: Penguin Books, 2008.

Bennett, Gordon D., and Jeffrey C. Patton, eds. *A Geography of the Carolinas*. Boone, NC: Parkway Publishers, Inc., 2008.

Brown, Dr. Russell K., and Vicki H. Greene, eds. *From Greenhouses to Green Jackets—Some History and Personalities of the Augusta National Golf Club*. Augusta, GA: Richmond County Historical Society, 2003.

Chernow, Ron. *George Washington—A Life*. New York: Penguin Press, 2010.

Clotworthy, William G. *In the Footsteps of George Washington*. Blacksburg, VA: McDonald & Woodward Publishing Company, 2002.

Earley, Lawrence S. *Looking for Longleaf—The Fall and Rise of an American Forest*. Chapel Hill: University of North Carolina Press, 2004.

Ellis, Richard. *Presidential Travel: The Journey from George Washington to George W. Bush*. Lawrence: University Press of Kansas, 2008.

Freeman, Douglas Southall. *George Washington: Patriot and President*. Vol. 6. New York: Charles Scribner's Sons, 1954.

Gessler, Diana Hollingsworth. *Very Charleston*. Chapel Hill, NC: Algonquin Books, 2003.

Grizzard, Frank, Jr. *George! A Guide to All Things Washington*. Buena Vista, VA: Mariner Publishing, 2005.

Hagemann, James. *The Heritage of Virginia: The Story of Place Names in the Old Dominion*. 2nd ed. West Chester, PA: Whitford Press, 1988.

Hale, Louise Closser, and Walter Hale. *We Discover the Old Dominion*. New York: Dodd, Mead & Company, 1916.

Hall, Basil. *Chastellux's Travels in North America—In the Years 1780–81–82*. Carlisle, MA: Applewood Books, 1828. Reprint.

Henderson, Archibald. *Washington's Southern Tour*. New York: Houghton Mifflin Company, 1923.

Henriques, Peter. *America's First President: George Washington*. Fort Washington, PA: Eastern National Park Famous American Series, 2002.

Higginbotham, Don. *George Washington: Uniting a Nation*. Lanham, MD: Rowman & Littlefield Publishers, Inc., 2002.

Jackson, Donald, and Dorothy Twohig, eds. *The Diaries of George Washington, January 1790–December 1799*. Vol. 6. Charlottesville: University Press of Virginia, 1979.

Jefferson, Thomas. *Notes on the State of Virginia*. Chapel Hill: University of North Carolina Press, 1955. Originally published in 1787.

Johnson, Gerald W. *Mount Vernon: The Story of a Shrine*. Mount Vernon, VA: Mount Vernon Ladies' Association, 2002.

Kimball, Fiske. *The Capitol of Virginia*. Richmond: Virginia State Library and Archives, 1989.

Lipscomb, Terry W. *South Carolina in 1791: George Washington's Southern Tour*. Columbia: South Carolina Department of Archives and History, 1993.

Matthews, Albert, ed. *The Journals of William Loughton Smith, 1790–1791*. From the proceedings of the Massachusetts Historical Society, October 1917. Cambridge, MA: The University Press, 1917.

Moore, Margaret H. *Complete Charleston: A Guide to the Architecture, History and Gardens of Charleston and the Low Country*. Charleston, SC: TM Photography, 2000.

Morrison, Hugh. *Early American Architecture*. New York: Dover Publications, 1987. Reprint of 1952 Oxford University Press edition.

Powell, William S., and Michael Hill, eds. *The North Carolina Gazetteer*. 2nd ed. Chapel Hill: University of North Carolina Press, 2010.

Schemmel, William. *Georgia Curiosities*. Guilford, CT: Globe Pequot Press, 2003.

Smith, Perry M. *A Hero Among Heroes: Jimmie Dyess and the 4th Marine Division*. Quantico, VA: Marine Corps Association, 1998.

Smith, Richard Norton. *Patriarch*. New York: Houghton Mifflin Company, 1993.

Stone, Walter. *A Walk Through Old Salem*. Winston-Salem, NC: John F. Blair, 2000.

Suggested Readings

Tebbel, John. *George Washington's America*. New York: E.P. Dutton and Company, Inc., 1954.

Toledano, Roulhac. *The Natural Trust Guide to Savannah Architectural and Cultural Treasures*. New York: John Wiley & Sons, Inc., 1997.

Turner, Walter R. *Paving Tobacco Road*. Raleigh: North Carolina Department of Cultural Resources, 2003.

Twohig, Dorothy, ed. *The Papers of George Washington, Presidential Series, December 1790–March 1791*. Vol. 7. Charlottesville: University Press of Virginia, 1998.

———. *The Papers of George Washington, Presidential Series, March–September 1791*. Vol. 8. Charlottesville: University Press of Virginia, 1999.

Weeks, Christopher. *AIA Guide to the Architecture of Washington, DC*. Baltimore: Johns Hopkins University Press, 1994.

Highway Historical Marker Guidebooks

Andrew, Judith M., ed. *South Carolina Historical Marker Guide*. 2nd ed. Columbia: South Carolina Department of Archives and History, 1998.

Hill, Michael, ed. *Guide to North Carolina Highway Historical Markers*. 9th ed. Raleigh: Division of Archives and History, 2001.

Salmon, John S., ed. *A Guidebook to Virginia's Historical Markers*. Charlottesville: University Press of Virginia, 1994.

These Newspapers Reported on the Southern Tour of 1791

Augusta (GA) Chronicle
Columbian Centinel (Boston, MA)
Dunlap's American Daily Advertiser (Philadelphia, PA)
Gazette of the United States (Philadelphia, PA)
Maryland Journal (Baltimore, MD)

Additional

Researchers can visit the Moravian Archives in Old Salem, Winston-Salem, North Carolina. The archives maintains clippings, articles and photos of Washington's Southern Tour and a film of the 1932 Old Salem reenactment of Washington's 1791. Visit www.moravianarchives.org.

SUGGESTED READINGS

Travels of George Washington Map. Washington, D.C.: National Geographic Society, 1932. This map is still available for purchase.

INDEX

INDEX

About the Author

W arren L. Bingham is a writer, speaker and broadcaster with a deep interest in southern history and lore. A graduate of the University of North Carolina at Chapel Hill and of Hollins University in Roanoke, Virginia, Bingham lives in North Carolina with his wife, Laura, and a couple of hounds.